YES, PLEASE TELL ME!

JENNIFER M. SCHMIDT, M.ED
AND
MEGAN R. BARRETT, M.ED

(817) 277-0727
(817) 277-2270 (fax)
E-mail: info@fhautism.com
www.fhautism.com

Copyright © 2021 by Jennifer M. Schmidt, M.Ed and Megan R. Barrett, M.Ed

All rights reserved, including the right of reproduction in any form, or by any mechanical or electronic means including photocopying or recording, or by any information storage or retrieval system, in whole or in part in any form, and in any case not without the written permission of the author and publisher.

Names: Schmidt, Jennifer M., author. | Barrett, Megan R., author.
Title: "Yes, please tell me!" : using the PEERspective learning approach to help preteens navigate the social world / Jennifer M. Schmidt, Megan Barrett.
Identifiers: ISBN: 978-1-942197-69-0 (paperback)
Subjects: LCSH: Youth with autism spectrum disorders--Behavior modification--Study and teaching. | Autistic youth--Behavior modification--Study and teaching. | Autism spectrum disorders--Patients--Behavior modification--Study and teaching. | Asperger's syndrome--Patients--Behavior modification--Study and teaching. | Middle school students--Life skills guides--Study and teaching. | Preteens--Life skills guides--Study and teaching. | Social skills in adolescence--Study and teaching. | Social interaction in adolescence--Study and teaching. | Communicative competence--Study and teaching | Autism spectrum disorders--Patients--Life skills guides--Study and teaching. | Teachers of children with disabilities--Handbooks, manuals, etc.
Classification: LCC: RJ506.A9 S362 2021 | DDC: 618.92/858832--23

TABLE OF CONTENTS

Foreword v

Acknowledgements vii

Chapter 1: What is PEERspective? 1

Chapter 2: How does PEERspective work? 11

Chapter 3: How do I get my district on board? 18

Chapter 4: Where do parents fit in? 21

Chapter 5: Wow, we get to do that? 25

The Middle School PEERspective Curriculum

Unit 1: "How can I make friends?" 35
           Friendships, Rapport Building, and Trust 35

Unit 2: "Where do these rules come from?" 55
           Anticipated Middle School Behaviors 55

Unit 3: "What if things don't go my way?" 73
           Dealing with Setbacks and Change 73

Unit 4: "How do I keep it all straight?" 94
           Executive Functioning 94

Unit 5: "It's All About Perspective!" 116
           Using a Filter and Thinking Socially 116

Unit 6: "Instagram is real, right?" 140
           Navigating Social Media in Middle School 140

Unit 7: "Why can't I do that anymore?" 156
           Growing Up, Changing Rules, and Transition 156

Unit 8: "We get to watch a movie?" 181
           Using Film and Video Clips to Teach Social Skills 181

References 213

Appendices 221

Acknowledgments and Collaborations 249

All unit handouts and appendices may be downloaded from https://drive.google.com/drive/u/0/folders/0AL6AlagLxfDFUk9PVA.

FOREWORD

"Ah, middle school—those were the days," said no one, EVER (p. 1).

When I read this sentence, I knew this book was special. And I was correct. Jennifer Schmidt, with the help of co-author Megan Barrett, has written another excellent book about helping students meet their potential.

The Office for National Statistics (2021) in the United Kingdom recently released data showing that only 22% of autistic adults have *any kind* of employment. This is in comparison with people with other disabilities who have an employment rate of 52% and those without disabilities of whom over 80% are employed. This same study revealed that a large percent of autistics experience anxiety, loneliness, and a deflated sense of well-being.

Why? Why do autistic people – who, like anyone have limitless potential – lack access to these basics of life? The reasons are many and the solutions are often complex.

One of the barriers to a high quality of life for people with autism is instruction with support – specifically in the area of social communication. We know this is important to life success for autistics, yet schools do not often provide social communication classes. It seems that schools expect autistic students to absorb social communication skills from their environment – something that most of us know is nonsensical.

I first met Jennifer Schmidt when she published "Why Didn't They Just Say That: Teaching Secondary Autistic Students to Decode the Social World Using PEERspective: A Complete Curriculum. PEERspective teaches self-awareness, self-acceptance, relationship building, conflict resolution, managing stress and wellness, and many other topics that have a lifelong impact on students. It has made a significant difference in the lives of many autistic and neurotypical high school students.

This book, "Yes, Tell Me Please" is a much needed prequel. The middle school PEERspective addresses so many of the social communication (friendship) challenges experienced by middle school students. It's real world, commonsense approach is backed by research and a strong knowledge of what middle schoolers need to learn, want to learn, and how they want to learn! A trifecta for success. This book, to quote a cliché, "is a must have."

Imagine a world where students have access to PEERspective in middle school and high school. This investment in student social communication development will lead to success in college, work, and community! It may be the pivotal point that allows our students to become the leaders that they deserve to be!!!

Well done Jen and Megan!

Brenda Smith Myles, Ph.D.
Researcher, consultant, and author of many books on autism spectrum disorder

Office for National Statistics (2021). Outcomes for disabled persons in the UK. Retrieved October 16, 2021 from https://www.autism.org.uk/what-we-do/news/new-data-on-the-autism-employment-gap.

ACKNOWLEDGMENTS

Our book states that this was written "with Sara Anderson" because Sara has been an integral part of the writing process with this book, as well as Jen's first book, *Why Didn't They Just Say That?* Sara's insight, talent, and patience through this process has helped to make this book convey the passion we each have for this field. Thank you for being a part of this journey, Sara; we are both incredibly grateful.

We also want to say a big thank you to Brenda Smith-Myles for taking time out of her busy schedule to not only write the foreword for this book, but to also give us insight and advice along the way. We appreciate her working with us early in the process to help guide our vision and get these vital lessons into the hands of educators and therapists around the world. Brenda has always believed in the PEERspective Learning Approach and continues to advocate for intentional social skill intervention for people with autism so they can meet their true potential and live a fulfilling life.

Pame Ferguson serves as a paraprofessional for the middle school class in which this program was first used, and has our gratitude for being supportive in every way possible with the implementation of this class model at the middle school level. Paraprofessionals do not hear enough the amazing credit that they deserve. Pame, you are an intricate piece of this process that has made it the suc-cess it is. Thank you for always being willing to step up, work to problem solve, and supporting our vision for the success of our students.

This curriculum would not be possible without the support of our amazing team of administrators. Paul Otten and Bobbie Fiori, thank you for trusting us to implement this program within our school district for a group of students who are often lost in the shuffle. Trisha Rahe and Allison France, thank you for taking the initiative to find a way to address these student needs at our school, and for empowering us. You are always willing to find a way to support students and us as teachers, which is a huge part of our success. We are eternally grateful. Dale Wren and Brian Shimko, as the principals of the middle school at the time, thank you for believing in this curriculum and supporting it to the fullest extent possible. We know that your belief in the program helped to create buy-in for many students, teachers, and parents within our community, and that has helped the program continue to grow and become the success it is today.

Furthermore, many of the ideas in our book have been contributed by others who support our vision. Thank you to the following passionate educators who contributed to the success of our program and this book through their thoughtfully constructed lessons; we are eternally grateful for your friendship and we love to collaborate with each of you: Molly Klonk, Mary Yelton, Marcia Harris, Sarah Allworth, Rilie McKaig and Marina Mendel.

Without our wonderful students and their supportive families, our ideas would still simply be just ideas; thank you for trusting us with your students and trusting in this process. While many of you have shared ways this class has made a difference in your lives and helped you to be successful, we want you to know that you have always made such a difference in our lives. You, our students, are why we do what we do and why we are so passionate about our work. Thank you for taking the opportunity to be involved in this curriculum, and believing in it's potential. A special thanks goes out to 2020-2021 BHS PEERspective students for helping with the video clips, and to Mackenzie Binkis and Alison Stonecypher, the student artists featured in this book, along with BHS PEERspective alum (and Jen's daughter), Elyse Schmidt and Danielle Brooks from Style House Photography for the amazing headshot photographs.

Finally, we both want to thank our friends and families for their endless support of this endeavour and the extra time we spend with our students on social outings that take away from our time with our loved ones. Thank you all for understanding that this work is a passion and that we are blessed to do it. Oprah Winfrey has said, "Surround yourself only with people who are going to lift you higher." We thank each of you for helping lift us as we continue to do this important work. Our students and their families deserve it, but we are well aware of the fact that we could not do this without each of you.

CHAPTER 1
WHAT IS PEERSPECTIVE?

"Ah, middle school—those were the days," said no one, EVER. Most of us probably agree that middle school was, well, rough, to say the least. I can not-so-fondly remember an awkward middle school me, bad perm (that's what happens when your mom is a hairdresser), uniform socks pulled up to my knees (Catholic school mandate), trying to find out who I was and where I fit in. If those of us who generally navigate the social world innately struggled in middle school, then it´s no wonder our students with autism do, too.

Since we all know that middle school can be a challenging social time for all students, it came as no surprise when our district approached me, Jen, about trying out the PEERspective model at one of our middle schools. The students there experienced similar challenges as the high school students with autism for whom the class was originally designed. These amazing individuals were having difficulty understanding their peers' and teachers' intentions, unwritten social rules, and how to communicate and get along with others. I knew the model would work at the middle school level but thought it would take a couple of years to catch on and make a difference. I was uncertain that younger students would be mature enough to support other students with autism and teach them to navigate socially, both in middle school and beyond.

As with most of my hypotheses, I was so wrong. Under the guidance of Megan Barrett, my co-author, the class took off right from the start, and the school climate began to shift and change. Students who ate lunch alone or in a classroom away from others now had friends to spend time with. Attendance records improved, grades went up, and the students with autism seemed much happier and integrated themselves into the school community more regularly. A staff poll was conducted at the end of the middle school pilot year, and 100 percent of those surveyed (teachers, counselors, principals, and other school personnel) said they felt the class had a positive impact on the students and overall school community.

> Social Communications Class [based on the PEERspective model] provides support for students who struggle with how to handle the complexities of social interactions that we sometimes take for granted. [Megan's] leadership in this new role, combined with the help of over a dozen peer models, had an immediate impact on the culture at Ankeney. It has created connections between students that would not have occurred otherwise. It has created understanding and empathy. And most importantly, it has created a sense of belonging for students who have long been trying to find their niche.
>
> —Dale Wren, Principal, Ankeney Middle School

Even after 24 years in the classroom, I still am learning, but in the process, I have made an important discovery: how to help students with autism learn to better associate with their world. We hope that by sharing our experiences and class model, we'll help others implement PEERspective in their schools. Megan and I are confident that this new approach will help your students to decode the social world and eventually see their autism as the gift it can be.

Megan once shared with me a story about one of our favorite students—don't even try to pretend you don't have favorites! This young lady, Helen, struggled greatly her first two years of middle school and was one of the catapulting reasons for piloting a middle school PEERspective class. Although Helen was very bright and musically gifted, her grades and attendance record didn't reflect her ability. She had missed more than 75 days of school during her 7th grade year and would scramble to catch up on her missing work upon her return. Beyond these academic struggles, when she was at school, Helen spent a lot of time in the office with both counselors and principals. Most of the incidents were due to lack of a filter or not understanding social nuances. Here is that story, told by Megan:

> *It was a beautiful fall day in Ohio, the leaves were various shades of yellow and orange, and the weekend was coming soon. I not-so-jokingly told my class that Friday was my favorite day of the week, and the students joked back with me. Then, Helen decided to join in the fun and loudly announced, "Friday ... my second favorite F-word!" The speech-language pathologist (SLP) was walking by and heard this. She and I explained to Helen that this was not an appropriate comment to make, and Helen became visibly frustrated with this redirection. She then told us both (and the whole class) that she shouldn't be in trouble because she did, in fact, filter her thoughts. She loudly announced, "What do you want from me? I didn't say _____." You get the picture!*

As with so many of the comments that come from students with autism, she wasn't wrong. The problem is that although this "filtering" was a possible step in the right direction for Helen, she was not quite where she needed to be in acquiring social skills, such as filtering her thoughts, and this would continue to have an impact in her life long after she left middle school.

Awareness Matters

Social awareness can make or break a person's success in life. The ability to interact in social, occupational, and academic settings is fundamental for positive social outcomes and the development of emotional maturity (Denham et al., 2001). Though they are often brilliant, many people on the autism spectrum are unable to obtain or maintain jobs due largely to their inability to understand social norms, and they often have difficulty understanding how to interact in social relationships

(Myles & Simpson, 2001). In general, people don't lose jobs because they are incompetent; they lose jobs due to inappropriate use of social skills. Folkman (2013) found that employees who were let go typically had poor interpersonal skills and nobody to support them.

Without someone to coach and guide employees on the spectrum, they are often written off after merely one or two poor social encounters. It is not good enough to be a technical genius; you have to learn to communicate as well. Students with autism are often seen as rude and self-centered; lack of reciprocity and social awareness will do that to a person.

Social Implications

Along with the lack of reciprocity, most students with autism have made many other social mistakes along the way, have probably written off friends, and have almost always experienced bullying as a result of their lack of social awareness (Seaman, 2012). Close to half of all teenagers with an autism spectrum disorder (ASD) are bullied at school, according to a 2012 survey of parents by the *Chicago Tribune* (Seaman, 2012). This is much higher than the estimated 11 percent of kids in the general population who are bullied (Seaman, 2012). According to a study by Humphrey and Symes (2010), students with ASD are approximately three times more likely to be victims of bullying than students with dyslexia and students without identified disabilities. Furthermore, Humphrey and Symes (2010) found that students with ASD were the second most likely to be bullied, with students identified as having behavioral, emotional, and social difficulties being the most likely.

Students on the spectrum are easy targets. Their encounters with bullying go one of two ways: either the student just looks down and ignores the bully, or they become the poster child for good versus evil, inserting themselves into situations. Although well-intentioned, we have known students with autism to tell the teacher if they see a student asking for help from another student when the teacher instructed the class that there would be no talking.

According to the *Diagnostic and Statistical Manual of Mental Disorders (American Psychiatric Association, 2013)*, autism is a pragmatic (social) communication disorder. Specifically, people with autism have deficits in using communication for social purposes, impairments in the ability to change communication to match context, and difficulty following the rules for conversation; often, they cannot understand what is not explicitly stated. In addition, they are unaware of how their actions are perceived (Endow, 2016). The common impression that people on the spectrum do not care if people think they are rude is wrong. Instead, they sometimes appear that way because they cannot automatically identify and use social information.

Social awareness and social interaction skills are critical to successful social, emotional, and cognitive development (Bellini, 2006). As educators, therefore, it is imperative that we teach pragmatic language to students who might not reach their full potential in life if they are not taught how to play the "social game."

Meeting the Need

This all sounds great, but how do we teach social skills to students who are already in or approaching their teens?

Before designing PEERspective at the high school level 14 years ago, Cindy Brinson (the SLP) and I were frustrated that the social skills she taught in therapy and I reinforced in my small-group tutoring class were not generalizing to the students' other classroom settings. We decided to brainstorm and try various other approaches. In all fairness, we should not have been surprised at our lack of success, as research has shown that traditional social skills training programs are only minimally effective in teaching social skills to children and adolescents (Bellini, 2006; Gresham, Sugai, & Horner, 2001; Quinn, Kavale, Mathur, Rutherford, & Forness, 1999).

Eventually, we decided to try peer mentoring, also called peer-based intervention (Apple, Billingsley, & Schwartz, 2005; Bass & Mulick, 2007), whereby the teacher is more of a facilitator, and nondisabled peers who have been systematically taught to prompt and respond to the targeted students become the teachers; we refer to them as our peer coaches. Peer mediation is an effective strategy for facilitating social interactions with children with ASD, among other disabilities, and their nondisabled peers (Bellini, 2006; Laushey & Heflin, 2000; Odom, McConnell, & McEvoy, 1992; Sasso, Mundschenk, Melloy, & Casey, 1998; Strain & Odom, 1986).

I had used peers to facilitate social skills instruction and found this approach invaluable once rapport was established between the peers. We agreed that peer mediation was critical to our students mastering, transferring, and generalizing social skills for real impact in day-to-day life. Peer coaches need to be selected with care. They need to be plugged into the school community and be kind and empathetic. Empathy is important, but so is mutual respect. Students with autism don't need a "helper"; they need a peer coach who will mentor them through the process of learning pragmatic language during the course of a year.

Still, we knew that we were missing a critical component to effectively teaching social skills: time! Gresham et al. (2001) recommended that social skills training be implemented more frequently and more intensely than is typically the case. They concluded that 30 hours of instruction, spread over 10–12 weeks, is not enough (Bellini, 2006).

We clearly needed to spend more time on social skills; 10 to 20 minutes a week was simply not sufficient enough in time and intensity for mastery, and then generalization, of skills that are as complex and challenging for our students on the spectrum as chemistry or calculus might be to a neurotypical student. However, we were confronted with the challenges faced by most teachers: with ever-increasing demands for academic accountability along with dwindling resources, it is difficult to meet even the basic requirements of a modern curriculum.

Furthermore, our home state, Ohio, is among many states that have recently recommended social-emotional standards implemented into a student's daily curriculum. "In *Each Child, Our Future*, Ohio's Strategic Plan for Education, social-emotional learning (SEL) is one of four equal learning domains supporting Ohio's goal of preparing each student in Ohio for postsecondary life" (Ohio Department of Education, 2019). Ohio and other states are starting to recognize the importance of SEL and the impact these skills have on a student's future success. Nationally, the Collaborative for Academic, Social, and Emotional Learning (CASEL) has identified five core competencies of social-emotional learning that our lessons align with: self-awareness, self-management, social awareness, relationship skills, and responsible decision-making (2020); these competencies are all practiced in PEERspective. After each lesson, you will find the most relevant SEL competencies that the lesson activity focuses upon.

Fourteen years ago, Cindy and I wondered how we could make our ideas work and decided we wanted to start a social communication class, developing the PEERspective model. The first step in starting our own class was to get approval from the administration, but we suspected they would see the need for such an intervention as much as we did. After all, they were putting out fires all day long with many of our students with autism, and almost all of the perceived behavior issues really stemmed from pragmatic language deficits. Lack of social awareness and boundaries were usually to blame.

In the high school PEERspective curriculum outlined in *Why Didn't They Just Say That?* (Schmidt, 2017), topics such as trust/team building, self-acceptance, stress management, anger management, nonverbal communication, dating, resolving interpersonal conflict, self-advocacy, and life transitions are presented through fun, interactive lessons that integrate evidence-based practices (Wong et al., 2015).

Research indicates that in order for social skills to generalize, or carry over into other areas naturally, they must be practiced in authentic settings (Radley et al., 2014). To address this issue of authenticity, we decided that each quarter we would require the students to attend one field trip during school hours and one social outing outside of school hours. All outings and field trips would involve authentic school-aged activities, occurring at football games, dances, restaurants, bowling alleys, movies, or the mall. This would allow students to practice the skills in authentic, natural environments. Prior to each outing and field trip, we would discuss the event in detail and role-play different scenarios students might encounter.

In addition, using challenging assignments and a supplemental text is also helpful in confirming to the students and their parents that this is not a special education course. Nevertheless, we anticipated that convincing academically gifted students to take a class taught by a special educator might be difficult. While social skill deficits are a detriment to any student, this isn't always easy to explain to students or their parents. At the middle school level, students get such a limited number of elective classes that sometimes this is a factor. Megan found that, after a student was referred by their classroom teacher, the most effective way to get the student's parents on board was having a counselor reach out to them to explain the model and its effectiveness.

PEERspective

SCC peer coaches and students enjoying their first school dance together.

When we decided to implement the high school PEERspective class over 14 years ago, we submitted a formal proposal to our principal (Appendix 2), asked if we could pilot PEERspective for one year, and explained that we would collect data using the Autism Social Skills Profile (Bellini, 2006) (see Appendix 1). After obtaining initial approval, we decided to meet again toward the end of our pilot year and discuss the data collected, as well as anecdotal evidence.

Due to the previous implementation of this model at the high school level, this was not a necessary step for the middle school PEERspective class. Even if you are not required to prove the effectiveness or submit a proposal to start PEERspective, we would still highly recommend collecting pre and post data using the Bellini or another data collection model. Recently, the amazing Beavercreek City Schools' speech-language pathologists collaborated to create a data collection tool via Google Forms that you may find helpful. This is found in the *Yes, Please Tell Me* electronic resources. This tool allows you to collect data and see the impact PEERspective is having at your school!

As with the high school class, the first middle school class results exceeded our expectations; it quickly became apparent that the social skills we focused upon began to flow over into the students' other classes. Other teachers were noticing that the targeted students became more confident and seemed happier. They were trying new things and making friends. The parents also reported on the difference they were seeing at home. One student even observed, "Everything in this class has helped me to be in a better social life."

When we first implemented the class, we were thrilled we had found a way to help our students with autism; what we hadn't planned on was the lasting effect the class also had on the peer coaches.

They, too, gained confidence and assertiveness throughout the year and seemed to benefit from the curriculum just as much as the targeted students. All students became friends over the course of the year, not because we told them to, not because they were being nice, but because they had the opportunity to get to know some outstanding people on the spectrum.

With a population whose pragmatic language skill gains are minimal, as evidenced in the educational literature, we felt that we were on to something, and that is how our model came about. We are delighted to share the model with others and confident that this approach is effective and will make a difference in the lives of your students as well.

PEERspective: Frequently Used Evidence-Based Practices

The PEERspective program has proven to be an effective way of providing services to an underserved population. The combination of time, intentionality, peer coaches, authentic practice, and the frequently used evidence-based practices (EBPs) is what makes PEERspective work. In an effort to determine which interventions are most effective for students with ASD, the National Clearinghouse on Autism Evidence and Practice (NCAEP) applied a set of rigorous criteria to a series of interventions commonly used with this population of students. Twenty-seven interventions met the criteria as being effective with students with ASD when implemented correctly (Steinbrenner et al., 2020).

PEERspective incorporates many of the recognized EBPs into the daily curriculum, so it is no surprise to observe huge improvements in the performance and behaviors of participating students with autism, both inside and outside of school. The following chart highlights PEERspective's seven most commonly used EBPs; a more comprehensive list of EBPs used in our program is found in Jen's first book, *Why didn't they just say that?* (Schmidt, 2017). The chart below includes definitions, as well as a brief explanation of each, referred to as "Teacher Talk." Teacher Talk is straight talk from Jen and Megan—after all, they are in the classroom every day, like you!

Jen and Megan will share their thoughts with you in the book's Teacher Talk sections!

Evidence-Based Practice (EBP)	NCAEP definition (more concise)	How it is used in PEERspective	Teacher Talk
Modeling (MD)	Demonstration of a desired target behavior that results in use of the behavior by the learner and leads to the acquisition of the target behavior.	Peers serve as models throughout the year in a variety of settings. This includes drama, role-play, and authentic social settings, both inside the school building and during social outings. Teachers and peers demonstrate the desired behavior through MD, which then allows students with autism to replicate it in a variety of settings.	We all know the expression "Monkey see, monkey do," right? But honestly, the trained peer coaches are the most effective tool when utilizing modeling in a natural way that allows targeted students to see what is appropriate and socially accepted behavior.
Peer-Based Instruction and Intervention (PBII)	Intervention in which peers directly promote autistic children's social interactions and/or other individual learning goals, or the teacher/other adult organizes the social context (e.g., playgroups, social network groups, recess) and provides any necessary support (e.g., prompts, reinforcement) to the autistic children and their peer to engage in social interactions.	The PEERspective teachers train the peer coaches to provide social initiations and interactions. Lessons are designed to allow the peer coaches to then become the teachers. This occurs in activities such as group work, presentations, partner activities, and social events inside and outside the classroom setting.	Middle school students do not want their teacher instructing them on how to relate to their peers and socialize. Fostering opportunities to allow students to learn from their peers of the same age is an important part of the model.
Self-Management (SM)	Instruction focusing on learners discriminating between appropriate and inappropriate behaviors, accurately monitoring and recording their own behaviors, and rewarding themselves for behaving appropriately.	Students learn to stop and evaluate their behavior, especially social behavior, to reflect on if the behavior is appropriate or inappropriate. After becoming more aware of their behavior, the student can adjust their choices accordingly in order to earn the respect and attention of their peers. SM is often used with other EBP such as technology-mediated interventions, modeling, video modeling, and visual supports.	Most of the students we work with are not aware that their behavior is causing the people around them to have thoughts about them. Explaining the "why" behind self-management and the importance of monitoring and filtering their thoughts and behavior is the first step in making smart social decisions that can impact their relationships and their future.

Social Skills Training (SST)	Group or individual instruction designed to teach learners ways to appropriately and successfully participate in their interactions with others.	Our class model is based on the SST. The year-long class allows participants to build rapport and learn social skills in an intentional and immersive way. This helps students build better relationships.	SST is a building block of this model. It is an extremely immersive model focused on social skills acquisition. Students are engaged in the learning process and ready to participate and learn from their peers through lessons and authentic social practice.
Task Analysis (TA)	A process in which an activity or behavior is divided into small, manageable steps in order to assess and teach the skill. Other practices, such as reinforcement, video modeling, or time delay, are often used to facilitate acquisition of the smaller steps.	Some social situations are overwhelming; using a task analysis allows us to break down the steps to social success in a more manageable way in order to teach a specific skill and prepare a student for an upcoming social event or experience. TA is used throughout the school year to help ease anxiety when it comes to upcoming events and activities that many students may not be comfortable with doing immediately.	Let's relate this practice to loads of laundry: Doesn't the task feel less daunting when you break it up into multiple small piles, or even do just a little bit each day? This is how many of our students feel when they are practicing a new social skill. By breaking the skill down into more manageable steps, they find support and feel less anxious about trying new social things.
Video Modeling (VM)	A video-recorded demonstration of the targeted behavior or skill shown to the learner to assist learning or engaging in a desired behavior or skill.	Video modeling is used quite often in our class and helps targeted students to replicate appropriate and expected social behavior and interactions. By watching themselves or others doing a skill, they can acquire that skill and be successful.	VM is one of the most impactful tools for teaching social skills, so I encourage you to use it often! VM allows students to rewatch the desired behavior and is so much easier to implement than one might think. There are a variety of different types of VM, but one super easy way is to allow the students to record their role-play/drama. Trust me, the middle school students already know how to use the technology and may teach you a thing or two along the way. *(It can also be fun to have the students find their own video clips of desired social behavior. This can help you stay current with what is popular with your students!)*

Visual Supports (VS)	A visual display that supports the learner engaging in a desired behavior or skills independent of additional prompts.	We utilize many visual supports throughout the school year. Targeted students are often visual learners and prefer consistency and predictability. Visual tools help provide the supports and are easy to implement in any classroom setting.	Visual supports are such an essential tool used constantly in the classroom: something as small as a slip of paper reminding a student to complete a task, or an arranged daily schedule. Many different visual supports are available to help students acquire social skills and be more successful at using those skills throughout the school day.

As shown in the chart above, Megan and I use many evidence-based practices. PEERspective works because we have set up the class to include these EBPs; however, research aside, we want to talk to you teacher-to-teacher! Throughout the chapters, you'll see "Teacher Talk"—where we are talking directly to YOU. You are the teacher, therapist, or other service provider working with students with autism, and we want to be right alongside you on this journey.

This book is your step-by-step guide to implementing PEERspective in your district at the middle school level, or at the very least, an aid to allow you to start intentionally targeting social skills through the provided lesson plans. While the lesson plans are designed for middle school students, they can be modified for a variety of grade levels, settings, and ability levels. In Chapter 2, we will look at the steps involved in implementing PEERspective in your setting and show you how the PEERspective model is different.

CHAPTER 2
HOW DOES PEERSPECTIVE WORK?

Many schools have social skills programs, but the students are not generalizing the skills that are taught. PEERspective is a different way to teach social skills because it is more intentional. The power of this model is that the students learn social skills every day through peer-mediated instruction and intervention, and they practice what they learn in the school community with reinforcement from staff and peers, as well as outside the school in authentic social settings. PEERspective is intentional about teaching specific social skills and immersive in and out of the school, using many evidence-based practices for students with autism. As you plan to implement PEERspective at your school, or with your students in other settings, use the following questions to guide you in setting up the program as an actual class:

- How long is the course?
- How is the course graded?
- Who will teach the course?
- How can PEERspective work in nontraditional learning environments?
- Can the program be adapted for other learning environments?

Each school is unique, so you will have to work with your administrators to discover what delivery methods are the best fit for your students and school environment.

Students working together to create their own gingerbread house design during the holiday!

For the past four years as a speech-language pathologist, I have worked with a variety of students with social communication challenges by conducting direct small group instruction and indirect social groups such as Lunch Bunch and Communication Club. In 2018, I had the opportunity to attend an in-service in which Jennifer Schmidt presented a novel and intriguing way to assist students in transferring social communication and life skills learned in the classroom into the home, workplace, and community. I realized at the in-service that Jennifer's curriculum was the critical piece I had been looking for to further assist my students. I am excited to pilot the PEERspective curriculum, and I hope to incorporate the PEERspective curriculum into our middle school in the near future.

—Danielle Brodnick

How Long Is the Course?

The class can be offered as either a semester-long or a year-long course. Each session is an entire class period, which typically runs 45–60 minutes. Whatever length you choose obviously impacts how much content you can cover.

How Is the Course Graded?

Students are more likely to buy into the lessons if the class is earning them a grade. If you want to attract some of your school's more academically-minded peer coaches (along with a mix of other students who may not be as high-achieving), using a grade can be important. Also, the students on the spectrum are often very grade-driven so using an actual letter grade can help create buy-in from them and from their parents too. If the class does not hold academic value for all involved, it is not seen as a priority to the students or parents.

Teacher Talk

Giving a grade is a factor that must be considered carefully. If the class does not hold academic value for all involved, it is not seen as a priority to the students or parents.

Who Will Teach the Course?

The guidelines for teacher qualification requirements and class coding vary by state, so you will need to work with your administrators on this. While staffing in your school or district will play a large role in the approach you choose, the benefits of co-teaching the class versus having just one teacher should weigh heavily into the final decision. The preferred model is when the class is co-taught by a special education teacher and a speech-language pathologist (SLP). The SLP looks at things through a therapist's lens, whereas the special educator is trained as a teacher. These two points of view are a powerful combination both in the classroom and in planning for lessons and writing data-driven IEP goals. For example, the pilot middle school class was taught by a special education teacher with a paraprofessional's daily assistance and consultation from the SLP, occupational therapist, and autism specialist.

When a special educator and an SLP co-teach, the traditional speech pull-out setting is integrated with a resource room/general education setting. This setup is ideal. Unfortunately, SLPs are often spread very thin and may not be able to balance their pull-out therapy with co-teaching. If so, it is still recommended that the therapist help plan and come to class as much as possible. We recommend the SLP attend class on a consistent schedule so the students expect them and are not distracted by their presence. In the co-teaching model, we also recommend the SLP lead teaches some lessons and does not pull students out of PEERspective for any individual therapy.

Can PEERspective Work in Nontraditional Learning Environments?

While it would be ideal for every school to offer intensive social skills intervention through PEERspective, sometimes you have to start small. If your school is not in a position to offer a semester-long or year-long class, social skills lessons can still be integrated into various disciplines with the help of a peer model. If you show progress through these easily implemented strategies, then you can propose piloting your own class.

Providing opportunities for students to succeed in social interactions, both in and out of the classroom, is a positive step toward improved social skills training. Just by having students work collaboratively on projects or lessons, you are fostering social communication. When students are allowed and encouraged to take chances, they can eventually overcome their fears and become confident as they learn to push themselves beyond their comfort zone. Since students on the spectrum tend to be visual learners, positive social memories can cultivate confidence and generalize into other areas of their lives. If students "see" or remember themselves having successful social interactions through visualizing past social success, they are more likely to do it again.

Social skills can be worked on in any discipline using a variety of methods. For example, you can require students to present their work to the rest of the class individually, in pairs, or in groups. You might start the year by having students present in groups, then progress to presenting in pairs, and then require individual presentations by the end of the year. Furthermore, in any subject area, playing games is an easy and fun way to get students to interact and socialize. Games can be relevant to the curriculum or just for fun as a reward for positive behavior. You might do a few "Game Days" throughout the year where students are allowed to play games that they choose. The only rules are that the game must be approved by the teacher and that everyone must actively participate.

Games teach turn-taking, empathy (through taking on others' perspectives), sportsmanship, teamwork, compromise, and a multitude of other life skills that are vital to effective social interaction and, eventually, job success (Fenaughty, 2014). When you let students play games, they may think you are just being nice by letting them have fun, but in reality, they are practicing essential social skills that will benefit them beyond the classroom.

Social Communication Club

The Social Communication Club enjoys a local pumpkin patch and hayride on a social outing in the fall.

Miguel could barely control his excitement. "I can't believe I am going to the luau tonight!" The students in the Social Communication Club (SCC) were all attending the dance after school. This was not Miguel's first experience with after-school dances, and the previous one had not gone well. The difference was that this time he had support and would be attending with a group of friends from SCC, instead of going alone. This luau was much more than just straw skirts and flower leis; it was a way for Miguel to experience a positive memory. This would be a big part of helping him create a new social future.

Teaching and practicing social skills does not have to occur during school hours. Student clubs are another way to foster positive communication skills. If students have negative social experiences, then their social confidence goes down, but the reverse is also true. Social success leads to social confidence.

In a social communication club, students practice the various social skills taught in class in a more authentic setting. Students can seemingly master a skill within the four walls of a classroom, but does it really matter if they can't do it in the real world? This club creates an opportunity for great socialization practice and allows for community support. Some examples of these activities include attending school-sponsored extracurricular events such as sporting events, school plays, concerts, dances, and club meetings, touring local museums, visiting a variety of dining establishments, and holding student-hosted events in their homes.

While we encourage the PEERspective students to take part in the club, it is not required. SCC outings enable students to interact with other students they know from class while also meeting new people. Furthermore, they allow students who have already taken the class to continue practicing their social skills with friends.

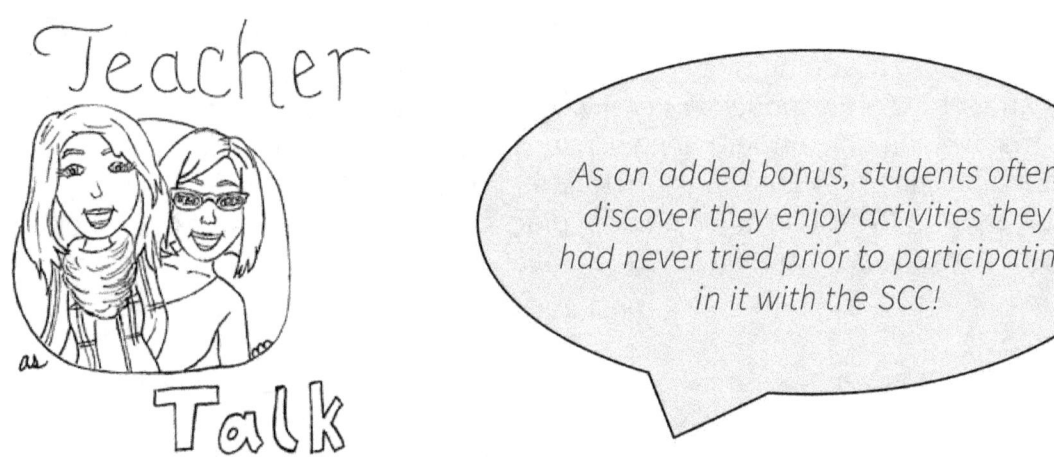

As an added bonus, students often discover they enjoy activities they had never tried prior to participating in it with the SCC!

Starting a social club may be a precursor to starting PEERspective, or it may allow you to provide authentic social practice where all students can experience positive social interactions beyond the confines of the school day. However, before these things can occur, you have to get your administration on board. That process is outlined in Chapter 3, so keep reading!

Adapting PEERspective for Other Learning Environments

While my initial work with PEERspective occurred in a traditional classroom, a number of other approaches could be used to incorporate the strategies in other learning environments. The first book in this series, *Why Didn't They Just Say That?* (2017) won a National Parenting Product Award in 2018, proving that this model is effective for use by parents as well as school professionals.

Homeschool and E-Learning

Provided your homeschool setting includes more than one student, it is completely possible to incorporate PEERspective social skills strategies into your curriculum. Parents have mentioned using the model and lessons in a homeschool environment, with siblings as the peer coaches. Often students that are homeschooled belong to a network where students interact with each other socially and/or take some classes together. This is another opportunity to implement the PEERspective model. As the COVID-19 pandemic taught us, having adaptable resources ready for nontraditional learning is always necessary. Everything in this book is easily accessible and well-organized in Google Drive; therefore, this model can easily be adopted in nontraditional classroom environments for online learning.

The curriculum from the first book in this series, *Why Didn't They Just Say That?* (2017), has been used as a homeschooling or e-learning curriculum, but that thought was not even on my radar. However, due to the nationwide closure of schools at the onset of the COVID-19 pandemic, having this type of curriculum on hand has become more important than ever. With the e-learning brought on by the pandemic, we discovered that many of the lessons in the PEERspective series lend themselves to both homeschool lessons and e-learning environments with some minor tweaking. This book has the added benefit of also providing an easily accessible and well-organized Google Drive to facilitate teaching it in any setting. This model can easily be adopted in nontraditional classroom environments. While that wouldn't hit a true "peerspective, it could still provide value, start conversations, and open communication (while having structure and an alternative to video games.)" (Cdaughe, 2018). Appendices 9 and 10 include other ideas for practicing social skills at home or in nontraditional learning environments. Practicing social skills in authentic ways is vital to generalizing these vital skills.

Never underestimate the power of playing games, it's a sneaky way to cultivate social interactions (in and out of the classroom).

As one review of *Why Didn't They Just Say That? (*Schmidt, 2017) stated: "I feel it could be utilized in 'homemade' social skills groups … if you have a group of ASD friends with siblings who could interact. (assign siblings to other kids, not their brother or sister). I think it could also be used with caregivers/babysitters for daily activities to try, especially if they are other teenagers. While that wouldn't hit a true "Peerspective," it could still provide value, start conversations, and open communication (while having structure and an alternative to video games)."

Many states are now requiring SEL curriculum, realizing that these skills are just as important as core curriculum, or dare I say even more vital! Math, for example, is used in many jobs, but not *all* jobs. Social skills and communication, though, are used in all jobs and all aspects of life. Social skills training is important in any classroom setting to help students develop social competence—the ability to engage in social interactions, establish and maintain relationships, and communicate needs and wants across contexts (Merrell & Gimpel, 1998; Stichter, Randolph, Gage, & Schmidt, 2007). Students who do not demonstrate social competence risk rejection by peers, academic failure, social dissatisfaction, and poor social perception (Alwell & Cobb, 2009; Sherman, Rasmussen, & Baydala, 2008). They may also experience negative long-term outcomes, such as difficulty maintaining relationships, staying employed, and developing outside interests (Eaves & Ho, 2008; Stichter, Conroy, & Kauffman, 2007).

CHAPTER 3

HOW DO I GET MY DISTRICT ON BOARD?

PEERspective is your opportunity to try a new way of offering social skills training to students with autism, social anxieties, or behavior that interferes with learning.

Seventh-grader Ari was an easy target for bullies. Despite the teachers' best efforts, a group of boys would sometimes try to push his buttons and get a reaction. One day, the boys told Ari, "You are not even a boy!" In Ari's literal mind, this was an easy thing to prove, and he did indeed prove them wrong, right there in band class. Obviously, this landed Ari in the office and took up quite a bit of the administrator's day.

Students who do not understand the social world can unintentionally end up in the office. Many administrators struggle to help these students and their parents understand the implications of these visits. While autism awareness is often at the forefront of the news, school personnel, while well-intentioned, may or may not be prepared to work effectively with these students and their parents. Getting administrators to buy into PEERspective isn't as difficult as you may think, as they are often putting out fires involving well-meaning students like Ari.

Identify Need

As you plan your proposal, it may be helpful to find out how many students with ASD are enrolled in your school and/or district. This information is available through the data collection system your state uses, which is reported by your district. In addition to these figures, you might ask your school's SLP for a list of students who would benefit from the program. We also suggest you ask fellow teachers, both special and general educators, because some targeted students may not have disclosed a disability but could still benefit from inclusion in your class. Appendix 4 includes a checklist you can ask teachers to fill out to identify potential students.

Course Proposal

After you have identified students who will benefit from the class, you need to plan your approach. Start with one class period (usually 45–50 minutes every school day). Next, you need to decide on the delivery model you will use: will you co-teach with an SLP, paraprofessional, or special education teacher, or are you going to do it alone?

As you work on your proposal, be sure to include the importance of field trips and outings so the students can practice skill generalization. Administrators are more likely to approve field trips if you explain their importance. To reduce costs at our school, we ask the district only for transportation costs; students pay their own costs for the field trip, such as entrance fees, meals, or games. Most parents support our efforts and do not mind this minimal expense; however, many activities could be organized with no cost to the students if asking families to contribute is not feasible: an after-school board game party, for example, or showing a movie on campus. Area businesses also have been willing to donate items to the class or at least give a discount. If even a minimal expense is a barrier in your school, some social opportunities might still be available, so don't give up. These group activities are a critical part of helping social skills generalize and cultivating rapport and relationships.

Another critical component of your proposal is the curriculum or syllabus (see Appendix 3), which allows your administration to get an idea of the type of class you are proposing to teach. PEERspective can be mistaken for a special education course. Although the class is taught by staff from the special services department, the curriculum is not special education. After you have completed these steps, you should feel confident that you have a strong proposal to submit to your administration for their approval.

Contact Parents

After you receive administrative approval, you are ready to begin! The next step is to send a letter of invitation to parents of potential student participants (see Appendix 5 for targeted students and Appendix 6 for the peer coaches). Parents should be clear about exactly what the class is designed for and why their child has been chosen. Most parents and students are thrilled to be part of our program. If parents are wary or unsure about having their child be a part of the program, after the benefits and curriculum specifics are explained, they typically see how the unique social aspects of PEERspective can provide solutions to many issues they have had in the past between school and home. Also, for many parents, the class has been a long-awaited solution to their student's struggles. They have tried countless other strategies with no success and are ready to find something that will work for their child to be a more active and successful individual within the school climate.

Once you have the class approved and students lined up, you are ready to begin changing your school for the better.

Impact on the School Community

In Beavercreek, students have been in classes with their peers with special needs since preschool, so for the most part, they are accepting and empathetic. Not all schools are as inclusive, and integrating students with autism into classes where they are academically challenged can prove difficult for teachers and students who are not as comfortable around students with special needs. The social communication class, based on the PEERspective model, can help shift and change the culture of classrooms and eventually the school climate. By training the peer coaches, you are teaching peers about the characteristics of autism and other social disorders, and you are creating not only allies for the targeted students but also eyes and ears throughout the school. Often coaches come to share an incident that happened in another setting so that the teacher can address it quickly to help the targeted student understand what happened and how to repair the situation.

While the program impacts students with autism in so many ways, it also provides a life changing impact for peer coaches as well. Coaches learn and discover a strong sense of empathy and compassion that leads many of them to successful careers and futures.

Nothing worth doing is ever easy, but in this chapter we have done the legwork for you. In addition to the steps outlined above, you will find all relevant materials in the appendices: a sample proposal that details the course for your administration (Appendix 2), sample syllabus (Appendix 3), data collection methods and suggestions (Appendix 4), and letters to parents inviting their student to participate in your class (Appendices 5 and 6).

CHAPTER 4
WHERE DO PARENTS FIT IN?

As educators, we know that parents play a vital role in their children's academic success. Social skills acquisition is no different from academics in that regard; actually, it could be even more dependent on parental support for success.

Mrs. Stoker was at her breaking point concerning the strategies used at the school for her son, Damien. As a student with autism, he was struggling with social skills, bullying, and a series of behaviors that were becoming problematic. She was so frustrated, she was ready to find alternative schooling options for her son. After a discussion explaining the social communication class model and topics addressed, a desperate Mrs. Stoker agreed to give it a shot. By the end of the school year, after a semester in the social communication class, Damien's behavior had improved at school, and Mrs. Stoker was also experiencing the success of the class with her son at home. Knowing the benefits of the class, she wanted to share the success she had had with her child with other parents in the community. She became a huge advocate for the class and ended up playing so many supportive roles, including hosting after-school outings, volunteering for field trips, becoming PTO president, leading other struggling families to the class, and speaking on behalf of the class about her family's personal successes.

After parents recognize the importance of intensive social skills intervention, it can be a hurdle for parents to trust that PEERspective is designed to help intentionally teach social skills through various teaching methods and academic rigor. While some parents, like Mrs. Stoker, are desperate to try anything, other parents might need more convincing to enroll their mainstreamed student in a class taught by a special educator. It is essential to explain that the class is based on research and uses 19 out of 27 evidence-based practices (Wong et al., 2015) for students with autism. Social skills goal-setting should be brought up at yearly IEP (individualized education plan) meetings so that parents understand that while this class is taught by a special educator, it is not a special education class.

Parent Meeting

It is preferable to wait until about a month into the school year to hold a parent meeting so that the students have started to make friends and talk about the class at home. This meeting allows parents to meet each other and learn about the program. You can explain the structure of the class, review the syllabus, and explain how peer mentoring works. You can discuss the importance of outings and field trips, emphasizing how these events push students out of their comfort zones and help them learn to generalize their skills. Reassure the parents that a teacher will be at the events and that students are only required to come and try. If a student decides to leave early, we applaud them for trying, as do the other students. As the year progresses, students tend to stay at outings longer and begin to enjoy going to school the next day and discussing their shared experience.

Parental Encouragement

As previously mentioned, many of our students have not had positive social experiences; thus, parents may hesitate to "make" them attend the field trips and outings associated with PEERspective. These authentic social experiences help the students generalize the social skills they are working on and are an essential part of the course. Again, it's important to communicate the "why" behind these fun outings. It's all about encouraging students to try something new and push themselves outside of their comfort zone. It can be scary for parents to trust that their child will have a good social experience! Over time, parents will see the benefits of encouraging their child to attend the social outings because they will come home from outings and field trips with the shared experience and positive social memories created, and their social skills will start to generalize to other settings that parents will observe. Often our students have not had many positive social experiences, so they do not understand why they should put themselves out there and try new things. Through positive social interactions, the students build rapport and social confidence to take with them into the next social outing!

Hosting and Volunteering Opportunities

Parent volunteers opened up their home to host a holiday party.

Mr. and Mrs. Chen hosted multiple PEERspective and SCC outings at their home which allowed the students to practice their social skills. They helped students tie-dye shirts in their garage (how brave is that?) and hosted game nights and movie nights for more than 30 students a multitude of times. One day, I was thanking Mrs. Chen for all she had done to support the class and club, and I will never forget her response. She said, "I believe in this class and what you are doing for these students. I feel this is my way of giving back to my daughter. I have done so much for my other three children but not for Lin because she never wanted to do anything social; she just wanted to hang out alone in her room. It is a blessing to get to host social things for all my children, even Lin, who is on the spectrum."

When parents host events, students become a part of the process. Students are often more comfortable in their own environment, so it can be a nice stepping stone to other social events. At the parent meeting, you should mention that you will be looking for parents to host or organize social outings throughout the year.

Even the parents of peer coaches find they are invested and want to actively volunteer in the social communication class. Once they see the purpose and the important role their child is playing, many of them reach out to help make the class successful through donations, volunteering, or becoming an advocate for the class.

Communication with parents is crucial. Not only can parents help support your class, but they can also reinforce the skills you are teaching. Parents can let you know how their children are doing at home and in the community. One of my favorite things is to hear from parents that they are noticing their child become more socially aware with friends and family. This type of open communication is really helpful because it gives insight into how the skills you are teaching are generalizing to other settings. If the parents notice improvements, that's a good sign.

CHAPTER 5
WOW, WE GET TO DO THAT?

As previously mentioned, the PEERspective model is a new way to teach social skill acquisition. Various components of the course are vital to the success and overall flow. These include peer models, field trips and social outings (authentic practice), book talks, and other environmental factors. Each teacher or therapist can choose how to integrate these components into their setting, but this chapter will share some of the most important (and fun) ways to intentionally teach social skills to your students.

Peer Modeling

Peer modeling is the most essential part of the program. Imitation is an early skill that serves a critical cognitive and social function in typical development (Uzgiris, 1981). We learn social skills by observing others, mimicking their actions, and then making these skills a part of our repertoire (Bandura, 1977b). While neurotypical students often do this with ease, most students on the spectrum fail to notice the social world around them and, therefore, miss out on this essential skill-building.

For some students with autism, the inability to pick up on social cues may be genetic (Risch et al., 2014). If students with ASD spend the bulk of their time with people who also struggle with social-emotional development, even if they are paying attention, they are not picking up on effective approaches to socialization.

Further, by the time students are eventually motivated to learn these important life skills, they are often older and have been the victims of bullying (Hebron & Humphrey, 2014). Thus, students with autism may tend to mistrust their peers—sometimes justifiably so. The result is motivated students who lack the opportunities to learn these skills because, traditionally, social skills are not taught in school. Besides, these students don't trust their peers, so they don't typically observe and learn these skills. It is a misconception that people with autism do not want to have friends or be social. A student once told me that he felt "alone in a crowd." I thought this was such an accurate description of how people often feel. Students with autism want to feel included and a part of what is going on; they just don't always know how to integrate themselves into a conversation or activity. This is why PEERspective is so important: this approach provides an intentionally safe and effective way for students to master life skills that will serve them now and in the future.

One aspect of PEERspective that has proven vital is the use of same-age peers. Peer-based instruction and intervention (PBII) is one of the 27 evidence-based practices for autism intervention (NCAEP, 2020) mentioned in Chapter 1 and forms the major underpinning of PEERspective. Our students don't want an "old" woman or man teaching them how to ask a friend if they want to go to the movies or hang out. They want advice from their peers who have gained their trust throughout the year. Peer coaches are often the best teachers in the room on any given day.

But much more is involved than just letting the students watch their neurotypical peers. Given the importance of peer modeling, it is essential to ensure that the peer coaches are carefully chosen and appropriately trained. Coaches should be students who are involved with their community and are well-liked within the student population. However, you should work hard to ensure that they are not the type of student who will be nice to your targeted student only when in class or around adults. In order to prepare coaches for the critical role they will play in PEERspective, the coaches attend a one-day session in the summer, usually the week before school starts. The goal of this session is to teach the basic characteristics of ASD and train the students how to be effective peer coaches.

As part of their training, it is important for the peers to understand that they are "coaches," not "helpers." Semantics matter, and it's likely that no middle schooler would willingly buy into having a helper. During the training (see sample agenda in Appendix 7), coaches are taught about the symptoms and implications often associated with ASD and how they can coach the targeted students through modeling and assertive, but kind, redirection. They also hear from past PEERspective participants—both coaches and students with ASD—and from parents of previous participants, to help them understand how important their role is and how this class can impact their own lives. They participate in a simulated activity about how it feels to have ASD, and they are treated to lunch so they can begin to build rapport with each other even before the school year starts. Finally, you should explain the structure of the class and remind them that not only are they coaches/mentors, they are taking the class for a grade.

Field Trips and Social Outings

Students attend a local dairy farm and learn more about the farm life and how to socialize with each other.

Without practice in authentic settings, students rarely use the social skills they learn in other settings without prompting and intervention (Bellini, Peters, Brenner, & Hopf, 2007; Ganz et al., 2012; Rao, Beidel, & Murray, 2008; Yakubova & Taber-Doughty, 2013). Since the goal is for students to be able to use these skills in their other classes, in the community, and at their future colleges and places of employment, practicing their skills in authentic settings is essential. So why is a field trip to the mall so educational? It is an authentic setting where many students will need to implement specific social skills with peers around them!

Field Trips

Within PEERspective, field trips occur once a quarter during school hours. The skills that students will use during these events are intentionally taught ahead of time, then observed and redirected during the event. In addition, following the field trip, the class debriefs about how the authentic practice went. At the end of the school year, we visit the mall, a typical hangout for middle school students, to practice social skills through a scavenger hunt activity; a sample questionnaire is included—see Unit 7, Lesson 6.

The field trips are designed to take the skills we have worked on in class and encourage skill generalization. The students are usually broken into groups on field trips, intentionally including target students and coaches together. We keep the pairing intentional and do not broadcast why the students are paired in a certain way. As a result of their training, the coaches understand that if we allow students to choose a partner to work with, they are to choose a targeted student. While it all depends on your population and group, most groupings are most successful at the middle school level with more guidance and decision-making from the teacher in terms of who should work with whom on field trips.

Other potential field trip ideas include lunch at a casual restaurant, miniature golf, bowling, or any other common middle school activity that allows the students to practice socialization.

Social Outings

Students attend a football game and wear their matching t-shirts!

Social outings follow a structure similar to field trips, but they happen after school hours. Many of my students with ASD have never been on social outings with peers, and at first, they have to push themselves outside their comfort zone to attend. But throughout the school year, they experience significant growth, and often by the end of the year they attend outings with ease. In fact, many students begin to participate in additional outings with friends and even host their own parties.

In the fall, we generally attend a school football game together. One of our students, Larry, had an eye-opening experience on this outing, which was his first football game:

Larry was not thrilled about this fall outing. In his mind, he was being forced by his parents to attend. "I don't even like football. What's the point of even going?" What Larry soon discovered was that attending a school football game isn't always about football. He had a great time at the game hanging out around the bleachers with his classmates, grabbing some yummy snacks at the concession stand, and not watching football.

Larry illustrates that you don't know if you like something until you try it. Nevertheless, many of the students end up deciding that they don't really like to attend football games, and that is fine; the goal is to give them a typical middle school social experience, not to convince them to like football. Also, this outing allows them to see that even if they didn't like the game, they still can feel proud of themselves for going. This social confidence and shared experience crack open the door to trying out the social world a little at a time.

Outings can be any event where students gather beyond the school day. Some possible outings include attending sporting events or plays, watching a movie, shopping, attending school dances, or going to gatherings hosted by students. These shared experiences help to build rapport and show students that the risk of putting themselves out there can result in friendships and acceptance.

When planning field trips and outings, there are a few things to consider. First, be sure that the event is authentic for the students and their age group. You want to help students have a positive social experience, and part of that is intentionality. Setting up field trips and outings is time-consuming, and it's important to communicate with the establishment and explain the purpose of the outing to anyone who may need to be extra patient with the students. If students are unable to pay for an outing, you can ask whether donations or discounts are available. It is useful to vary the type of outing—a meal out, a walk in the park, a school function (dance, play, sporting event). If the event is school-sponsored, free admission can usually be obtained. Finally, it's important to prime students for these activities in class prior to the event. You can use such activities as role-playing, talk analysis, video modeling, and showing pictures of what the students should expect when they attend the event. This can help ease the minds of students who may be hesitant to participate.

Don't hesitate to do a yearly fundraiser or ask local businesses to donate to your class or club in order to provide funds for field trips and outings!

Book Talks

Students enjoy morning breakfast treats and hot chocolate while sharing valuable information with one another.

Another way to help students have a shared experience and similar things to discuss is through Book Talks. While the image of middle-aged moms at Starbucks discussing novels might come to mind, our version of Book Talks is middle schoolers sitting at their desks arranged in a circle, discussing a book and enjoying a hot beverage—but with a grade attached. The students really enjoy this activity, and it lets them learn about social situations in a nonthreatening way, all while sharing their opinions and observations as they feel comfortable—see the Book Discussion Log in Unit 5, Lesson 2.

At the middle school level, our class reads the chapter as a whole group and discusses questions given prior to the book talk in smaller partner groups. On book discussion days, hot chocolate and breakfast items are provided. Students are divided into pairs and are responsible for grading each other's participation. You can vary the requirements, but we usually have each student share two comments or questions throughout the book talk. The partner setup allows the peer coaches to prompt their partner, along with allowing the targeted students to observe a model of how to meet the requirements by watching their partner. Book discussion days offer a relaxed change of pace from the day-to-day curriculum.

Book Selection

We have approached Book Talks in a number of ways. In the past, our school librarian helped us choose popular young adult titles that tied into the themes of the course. A potential middle school title to consider could be Michelle Garcia Winner and Pam Crooke's *Social Fortune and Fate* (2011). This book gets right to the heart of what we are teaching, which is the theory of mind (TOM)—the ability to understand and identify the thoughts, feelings, and interactions of others (Baron-Cohen, Tager-Flusberg, & Lombardo, 2013).

Takeaways

Takeaways, or ideas that students can take from a lesson and use in their lives, have proven quite helpful in driving home the big picture. By ending a lesson and or unit by focusing on the takeaway, students understand how our lessons and experiences in class can have a lasting impact on their lives. This is similar to using "exit tickets" to assess and obtain information about students' current levels of understanding and learning (Marzano, 2012). Often students with ASD perseverate on details, and the use of takeaways helps them master the content and see the big picture.

Many students on the spectrum lack TOM, which, in turn, adversely affects their interpersonal relationships and social interactions (Stichter, O'Connor, Herzog, Lierheimer, & McGhee, 2012). That is, they are often unaware of how their words and actions impact those around them. If you don't realize you are perceived as rude or mean, you are unable to change your behavior to get the desired outcome.

Over the years, countless students have come up to us with all kinds of social cue questions, often saying, "please tell me..." and needing further explanation on why certain social events occurred. Once the students start to grasp TOM, they can use this knowledge to adjust some of their behaviors and keep some thoughts and comments safely locked away in their "thought bubble." At the middle school level, our class has used several strategies to help students with their comments. Activities include comment cards and utilization of the acronym FOTO: Filtering out thoughts and opinions.

By filtering their thoughts and actions and utilizing TOM, students start to implement self-management, which is another recognized evidence-based practice (Steinbrenner et al., 2020). By learning self-awareness, they can monitor their behavior and make changes and adjustments as needed.

Classroom Environment

As educators, we strive to provide a comfortable learning atmosphere where all students can feel safe and learn. Below are some ways to do that.

Visual Supports

Among the many ways to accomplish this for students with ASD, Koul, Schlosser, and Sancibrian (2001) note that "clinicians and educators need to utilize a wide range of intervention strategies that can take advantage of visual modality in individuals with autism" (166). Visual stimuli can be used to teach a variety of social skills and provide students with concrete choices without having to rely on linguistic recall (Alberto, Cihak, & Gama, 2005; Bates, Cuvo, Miner, & Korabeck, 2001; Cihak, Alberto, Taber-Doughty, & Gama, 2006). For example, I use a board to post schedule changes and list the daily lesson plan where students can see it, and I employ a visual timer to aid students during activities.

These ideas may not seem groundbreaking, but visual supports—yet another example of an effective EBP (Steinbrenner et al., 2020)—can help students with ASD (and others) feel secure by providing structure and thereby lessening uncertainty and the anxiety that often comes with that.

Sensory Issues

Another way to create a positive classroom environment is to pay attention to the ambience of the room. Children with ASD tend to have hyper- or hypo-sensory responses to stimuli around them (Kientz & Dunn, 1997; Myles, Mahler, & Robbins, 2016), and such atypical sensory processing can negatively affect their functioning. For example, fluorescent lighting, common in many schools, can be bothersome from a sensory standpoint. Add the fact that dress codes often prevent students from pulling their hoods up or wearing hats to shade their eyes, and it is easy to understand why lighting can create sensory problems. If you cannot change or modify the lights, you may consider placing individual lamps around the classroom to use instead of turning on the overhead light, or simply turning on only one set of lights. Simple changes like this can have a large impact on creating a comfortable classroom environment.

Journaling

Journaling is another key component of PEERspective. Journaling is used almost daily in class and can be used at the beginning, middle, or end of class. Sometimes the journal prompt is to get the students thinking about the upcoming lesson; at other times it is to help them reflect on lessons and activities at the end of class. Regardless, journaling can be a helpful practice for students to process their thoughts by putting them on paper.

Journaling integrates cognitive behavior intervention (CBI) (Steinbrenner et al., 2020) into the class. CBI utilizes so-called cognitive restricting, which includes modifying how one thinks, feels, and behaves in order to improve social and behavioral outcomes. This, in turn, allows students to become more aware of themselves and others, which can improve social interactions and social confidence (Hart & Morgan 1993; March & Mulle, 1998; Reaven & Hepburn, 2003).

In PEERspective, journaling is followed by optional sharing time. As such, it can lead to some great teachable moments that would have been lost in the shuffle of my well-thought-out lesson plans, as illustrated in the following.

> *One day, after doing a lesson on unwritten rules in different environments throughout the school, a student named Cece wrote in her journal about lunchtime and how she typically left her lunch sitting on the table when she was finished. She figured that the custodian was there for a reason,*

and she might as well help him have something to do for his job. After writing down this example and sharing it in class, the peer coaches helped Cece to understand the negative thoughts that the custodian and other students may have about her when she leaves her trash sitting on the tables and heads out to recess. Hearing this information from another peer helped Cece to ensure that the next day, she gathered her trash and threw it away in the designated bin before heading out to play. What could have caused potential issues with other students and staff members ended up being a positive learning opportunity for Cece, thanks to the assistance of the journaling process and discussion with peers.

Parent Corner

This is included at the end of each unit as a wrap-up with your students and a way to share key concepts and vocabulary with parents. You can choose to modify the Parent Corner to cover the exact content you covered in the unit. You can also add a parent signature portion at the bottom of the page and have the students return the bottom portion of the form to make sure their parents did receive it, or you can email it. Having parents reinforce the concepts and vocabulary can be a vital part of skill generalization!

Staff Connection

You can modify the Parent Corner content to share with other staff members in your building. If they choose to use the same vocabulary you are using in PEERspective, students will quickly generalize these targeted skills and improve their peer relationships throughout the school community.

Students gather together for a group picture!

UNIT 1

"HOW CAN I MAKE FRIENDS?"
Friendships, Rapport Building, and Trust

It's no coincidence that friendship, rapport building, and trust are the first topics we cover, as these themes are embedded in many lessons throughout the course. We can require students to interact with each other when working in the classroom, but we cannot require the target students and peer coaches to trust each other immediately and build instant, meaningful friendships. Friendship and trust develop over time. What we can do, however, is spend time focused on building the foundation for friendships.

Carmen was excited for her very first middle school football game. With only two months of social communications class, she was finally making connections with classmates in ways she never had before. As she sat in the stands cheering on her fellow classmates, she was so excited to see one of our class peer coaches, a football cheerleader, cheering on the team! Her classmate took it upon herself to come up to the stands and give Carmen and a few other classmates school spirit t-shirts. What a night for Carmen! Not only did she get to attend her first football game and cheer on the team, she also got a free t-shirt. The natural friendships formed and comradery among students in the class was evident when they showed up the next day with a game plan to wear their shirts and match at school. Some students with autism have never had this type of close connection with other people or friends. This type of simple act can help create authentic bonds and show our students with autism that it can be worth it to push yourself outside your comfort zone in order to create relationships and how these relationships add value to their lives.

The friendships that evolve over the course of students' time together are built on mutual respect, shared experiences, intimate conversations, and purposeful cooperative learning. We are proud to say that many students remain friends after taking this course and have continued to the high school phase of their life and beyond with meaningful connections.

A former middle school peer coach, Piper Cullom, is now a high school student who is actively involved in her school community. Piper said, "As a member of the Social Communication Class family, I was so happy to have the whole class come to a football game to see our friend play football and me cheer. They cheered me and our friend on, even if they were not that interested in the game. This brought us together. We understood that we don't need to watch the game the whole time, we need to be there for each other. We learned that in order for this family to work we need to support one another, even if it puts us outside of our comfort zone. As a [peer] coach, I didn't feel like I was superior or better than my other peers, I felt as equals. This helped me grow and better communicate with new people, classmates, and my own siblings."

These relationships are not fabricated or forced; they happen when people are given the opportunity to be themselves and allow others to get to know them. When students experience social success, their confidence increases, and they become more willing to push themselves to try more new things and make even more friends. That's why exercises that emphasize trust and friendship are a vital part of the class.

Sadly, many students with ASD have had negative experiences trusting their peers. The rates of bullying among students with ASD are staggering. For example, a recent study conducted by the Interactive Autism Network (IAN) found that 63 percent of students ages 6 to 15 with ASD had been bullied at some point in their lives (Zablotsky, Bradshaw, Anderson, & Law, 2014). While people seem to be understanding and accepting when someone has an obvious physical disability, unfortunately, this is not so for students with autism—you don't get a free pass when you are in mainstream classes raising your hand more times than is socially acceptable, or arguing with the teacher because a collaborator on a group project didn't follow all of the rules required for the assignment.

According to the book *The Global Achievement Gap* (Wagner, 2008), seven skills for the 21st century promote future success for students. These historically underestimated skills include critical thinking and problem-solving; collaboration across networks and leading by influence; agility and adaptability; initiative and entrepreneurialism; effective oral and written communication; accessing and analyzing information; and curiosity and imagination. These vital life skills are interwoven into PEERspective units and lessons, helping prepare brilliant minds to shape and change the future.

While Unit 1 focuses specifically on trust, friendships, and building rapport, many of the lessons in this unit lend themselves to be integrated throughout the year. Building rapport is not just a first-quarter goal; it is something that is constant and can happen in many unique ways.

Specific lessons include:

- Straw Challenge
- Conversation Foundations
- Effective Conversations
- Friendship Collage
- Lyric Analysis

Unit 1: Friendships, Rapport Building, and Trust
Lesson 1: Straw Challenge

Materials, time allotted, and activity can vary based on your school resources and needs for this activity and others.

LESSON OBJECTIVES

1. Students will identify what productive group work looks like versus unproductive group work.
2. Students will effectively communicate their thoughts, ideas, and opinions with their group members.
3. Students will collaborate with peers to design and build a straw tower.

RATIONALE

During PEERspective, trust and communication are vital to the success of each student. The students need to know that they can work together and trust each other in order to complete a task or get through a problem together. In order to learn from each other, there must be mutual respect, which is built on trust and shared experiences. This activity provides these essential components and sets students up at the beginning of the year to understand group work expectations and trust among their classmates.

LESSON OVERVIEW AND INSTRUCTION

Lesson Duration

One 45-minute period

Lesson Materials

- 25–50 straws per group
- A roll of tape per group

Lesson Activity

1. Teacher divides students into groups of 4 to 5, with targeted students and peer coaches intentionally grouped together.

2. Teacher leads discussion of group work expectations and solicits answers from students about what productive group work looks like versus unproductive group work. Videos showing positive and negative group work strategies can be used to help provide a visual for effective group work.
3. Teacher explains the task to the students: they will work together to try to build the highest free-standing straw tower. They may plan and execute the task in any way they'd like, as long as the group, as a majority, agrees.
4. Groups are given 25 minutes to plan and execute their own straw tower.
5. At the end of the given time, the group with the highest tower receives a prize, the group that worked the best using the group expectations wins a prize, and the group that was most creative wins a prize.

Social Emotional Learning Competencies (CASEL, 2020) addressed in this lesson:

- Self-Awareness
- Self-Management
- Relationship Skills
- Social Awareness

SCC students work together to develop the sturdiest and tallest straw structure that they can!

Unit 1: Friendships, Rapport Building, and Trust
Lesson 2: Conversation Foundations

LESSON OBJECTIVES

1. Students will be able to determine acceptable guidelines for engaging in positive conversations with their peers, both independently and as a group.
2. Students will work together in small groups to create and implement a video script for meaningful conversations.
3. After filming and watching video scripts, students will contribute to a whole-class discussion about "takeaways" from their video scripts.
4. Students will take a summative assessment on conversation foundations after filming and class discussion.

RATIONALE

In this lesson, students will utilize class discussion and new information they have learned about having meaningful conversations and interactions with peers in order to create their own videos to display the foundations of good conversations. Students do this to get a better idea of helpful components of a meaningful interaction with peers. This lesson provides students with necessary visuals in order to help them understand a vital social skill concept. The discussion of conversation foundations helps students to go through a checklist in their heads and ensure that they are following their own class-created steps in having a conversation with their peers. The video modeling approach, which is used throughout this lesson, is a form of observational learning, in which desired behaviors are demonstrated (Steinbrenner et al., 2020). Targeted students thrive when given rules or expectations to help them succeed, so creating these ideas with their classmates helps them to take ownership of their foundations for conversations and use them in a realistic situation more frequently.

LESSON OVERVIEW AND INSTRUCTION

Lesson Duration

Two 45-minute periods

Lesson Materials

- Smartboard
- Student journals
- Writing utensils
- Internet for video clips (if wanting to provide visuals during group discussion)
- Filming device (iPad, video camera, etc.)

Lesson Activity

1. Students will utilize their journals and independently brainstorm 3 to 5 components for a good conversation and what a good conversation looks like.
2. They will then gather into groups with a mix of peer coaches and targeted students to determine their best 3 to 5 ideas that make up a strong foundation for good conversation.
3. Groups will share the 3 to 5 ideas that their group agreed upon, and then as a class, determine if that is an important part of meaningful conversations and interactions or not. The determination of the conversation foundation will take most of the first 45-minute period.
4. After determining the most important guidelines, students will work together in groups to create two video scripts: the first video should show bad foundations and negative actions when interacting in a conversation, and the second video should show positive foundations and desired actions that you would want to see to have a positive and meaningful conversation. These videos are typically one to two minutes long.
5. Once students have created a script and it has been approved, they may film it. They should film it in areas throughout school so that it is in an authentic setting.
6. After filming has taken place for all groups, the videos are compiled and played back for students to evaluate.

Social Emotional Learning Competencies (CASEL, 2020) addressed in this lesson:

- Self-Awareness
- Self-Management
- Relationship Skills
- Social Awareness

Unit 1: Friendships, Rapport Building, and Trust
Lesson 3: Effective Conversations

LESSON OBJECTIVES

1. Students will attentively watch the video and learn ten ways to have a better conversation.
2. Students will discuss their opinions in a respectful way.
3. Students will effectively communicate to their groups their thoughts, ideas, and opinions of the TED Talk.

RATIONALE

Using video clips helps create a common experience to discuss; some students have different success rates when entering into conversations with friends, family, and peers. It is easier to pick out the mistakes that others are making rather than our own. If we can recognize these mistakes in others, then we will be more aware of our own actions and how they might be perceived. This lesson defines the steps necessary to a good conversation in a concrete way that can be reinforced throughout the year by teachers and peer coaches.

LESSON OVERVIEW AND INSTRUCTION

Lesson Duration

One 45-minute period

Lesson Materials

- Smartboard, TV, or another way for students to watch video
- Paper journal for each student
- How to Have a Better Conversation handout
- Writing utensils

Lesson Activity

1. The students watch a TED Talk by Celeste Headlee that can be found online: https://www.youtube.com/watch?v=R1vskiVDwl4

2. As they watch, students will use the handout to record the different strategies she discusses that lead to better conversation.
3. After watching the video, students will break into small groups to discuss different ways they learned to have a better conversation.
4. Students then are given discussion questions about the video and how they can apply it to their lives to complete independently.
5. At the end of class, students participate in the whole-class discussion using their completed discussion questions.

Social Emotional Learning Competencies (CASEL, 2020) addressed in this lesson:

- Self-Awareness
- Self-Management
- Relationship Skills
- Social Awareness

TED Talk
How to Have a Better Conversation

Name_____ Date_____

List the ten strategies discussed in "10 Ways to Have a Better Conversation."

1. _____

2. _____

3. _____

4. _____

5. _____

6. _____

7. _____

8. _____

9. _____

10. _____

https://www.ted.com/talks/celeste_headlee_10_ways_to_have_a_better_conversation?language=en

Discussion Questions

1. Do you agree with all 10 of the tips on how to have a better conversation? Do you disagree with any? Explain why you agree or disagree.

2. Are there any specific tips you can imagine working on or improving on in your daily conversations with family, friends, or teachers?

3. Are there any tips that you can think of that you did or did not do this year at school or in other social situations?

4. What will these tips ultimately help you to do?

Unit 1: Friendships, Rapport Building, and Trust
Lesson 4: Friendship Collage

LESSON OBJECTIVES

1. Students will be able to brainstorm a list of characteristics that they look for in a friend.
2. Students will collaborate with other students in a small group.
3. Students will create their own "ideal" friend using the handout.
4. Students will present their "ideal" friend to their classmates at the end of the class period.

RATIONALE

Students will reflect on what characteristics make up an "ideal" or "good" friend. Through peer collaboration, students will construct a list of characteristics that would be socially appropriate for students their age. When completing the handout, the students' act of writing or creating their "friend" will reinforce the concept of what makes a good friend while using visual support. Having the students present their handout with the class incorporates public speaking skills as well.

LESSON OVERVIEW AND INSTRUCTION

Lesson Duration

One 45-minute period

Lesson Materials

- *What Do You Look For in a Friend?* Handout
- Markers or magazine clippings

Lesson Activity

1. Students are divided into groups of three to four students.
2. Group members will brainstorm a list of characteristics or qualities that they would like in a friend. Each group should generate a list of twenty characteristics and qualities, and then share two or three examples with the class.
3. Then, each student will be given a copy of the handout, *What Do You Look For in a Friend?*

4. Next, students will write their chosen characteristics on the handout to fill the figure. Or, instead of writing characteristics or qualities into the figure on the handout, students could cut out images from magazines to symbolize different characteristics or qualities.
5. Finally, each student presents their worksheet to the class.

Social Emotional Learning Competencies (CASEL, 2020) addressed in this lesson:

- Self-Awareness
- Relationship Skills
- Social Awareness

What Do I Look for in a Friend?

Name_____ Date_____

Unit 1: Friendships, Rapport Building, and Trust
Lesson 5: Lyric Analysis

LESSON OBJECTIVES

1. Students will be able to discuss different friendship experiences by completing the *Friendship Discussion Question* handout.
2. Students will be able to individually interpret the meaning of the song lyrics in "You've Got a Friend in Me."
3. Students will be able to personally reflect on friendship in their lives by completing the short response questions on the *Friendship Discussion Question* handout.

RATIONALE

Having the students reflect on personal experiences with their friends allows them to connect to the skills that they are learning. During the music video, the students are shown the lyrics as well as photos of iconic "friendship" moments in the movie *Toy Story*. The song "You've Got a Friend in Me" shares a great message in each stanza about what a good friend should do for someone. Finally, the short response questions require the students to make connections from their own friendships to concepts of being a good friend that are displayed in the song lyrics.

LESSON OVERVIEW AND INSTRUCTION

Lesson Duration

One 45-minute period

Lesson Materials

- Friendship Discussion Questions handout
- "You've Got a Friend in Me" song lyric handout
- Smartboard

Lesson Activity

1. The students will be divided into groups of 3 to 4 students. These groups will then complete the first four questions on the *Friendship Discussion Question* handout.

2. Upon completion of the handout, play the song "You've Got a Friend in Me." https://www.youtube.com/watch?v=zlYOJ_hSs0o
3. Students will then receive a copy of the "You've Got a Friend in Me" song lyric handout, where they will write and interpret different friend qualities from the song individually.
4. Then, students will complete the two short response questions on the *Friendship Discussion Question* handout and share their responses with their small group.
5. The entire class will come back together, and each group will share two or three takeaways from the activity.

Social Emotional Learning Competencies (CASEL, 2020) addressed in this lesson:

- Self-Awareness
- Relationship Skills
- Social Awareness

Friendship Discussion Questions

Name_____ Date_____

1. What do you like to do for fun with your friends?

2. How has a friend helped you through a tough time?

3. How are you a good friend to others?

4. What is the most important quality of a friend?

Please write about a specific time when you were a good friend to someone OR when someone was a good friend to you.
_____
_____
_____
_____
_____

What was your favorite song lyric and why?
_____
_____

"You've Got a Friend in Me"

Name_____ Date_____

Please read the song lyrics in the left-hand column and write down what you think they mean in the right-hand column.

Song Lyrics	Meaning
You've got a friend in me You've got a friend in me When the road looks rough ahead And you're miles and miles from your nice warm bed You just remember what your old pal said Boy, you've got a friend in me Yeah, you've got a friend in me	
You've got a friend in me You've got a friend in me You've got troubles, and I've got 'em too There isn't anything I wouldn't do for you We stick together and we see it through 'Cause you've got a friend in me You've got a friend in me	
Some other folks might be a little bit smarter than I am Bigger and stronger too, maybe But none of them will ever love you the way I do It's me and you, boy	
And as the years go by Our friendship will never die You're gonna see, it's our destiny You've got a friend in me You've got a friend in me You've got a friend in me	

Unit 1: Friendships, Rapport Building, and Trust

Additional Activities and Ideas

- **Guest Speakers:** Having past students come to share about their transition to high school can create a strong sense of community and allow the students to see how instrumental the class can be in their lives.

- **Ice Breakers and Name Games:** The students should feel connected to each other right from the start, and ice breaker games can help accomplish this—a quick internet search can lead to hundreds of ideas if you don't have any favorites. It is equally important for the students to learn each other's names early in the school year; name games can be a fun way to do both. You may want to have name cards for the students' desks for the first couple weeks to emphasize the importance and help the students learn each other's names quickly. This will hopefully prevent the "I'll work with the girl in the green shirt" problem that can ensue in the third quarter if you are not proactive about helping students feel connected early.

- **Game Day**: Game days are a great way for students to get to know each other and practice social skills while having fun. Be sure to approve all games before they play them in class. Some class favorites are Uno, Apples to Apples, and Pictionary.

- **Interview Assignment:** Have each student interview an adult (aunt, uncle, neighbor, parent) about how they met their best friend. Be sure to have them ask how they first met and how they maintain their friendship. Then, as a follow-up activity, create a class list of advice about how to make and maintain friendships.

Teacher name:
Teacher email:
Week of:

Parent Corner
Unit 1

Friendships, Rapport Building, and Trust

We covered the following concepts in Unit 1:

- **Trust and teamwork** is our first unit in PEERspective because the students have to learn to trust each other in order to build rapport and learn from each other.

- Tips for having a **better conversation** include:
  - **Don't multitask.** More than just setting your device aside—be present. Be in that moment.
  - **Don't pontificate.** Enter each conversation assuming that you can learn something new.
  - **Use open-ended questions.** Act like a journalist; don't go for easy yes/no responses.
  - **Go with the flow.** Let thoughts come and go. Follow the conversation, not what you thought the conversation would be like.
  - **If you don't know, say that you don't know.**
  - **Don't equate your experience with theirs.** Your experiences are never the same, no matter what the situation.
  - **Try not to repeat yourself.** Repeating yourself sounds condescending and creates boring conversations.
  - **Stay out of the weeds.** People don't care about the little details—the years, names, dates, etc. Leave them out.
  - **Listen.** This is the most important one.
  - **Be brief.**

- We talked about what it means to be a friend. Consider engaging your student in a conversation about what friendship means to them.

Next steps at home:

- Encourage your child to listen to their friends in PEERspective. Some of our students have not been treated well by peers, so creating authentic friendships in class can take some time.
- When you are having a conversation with your child, please prompt them to utilize the tips listed above; you may want to just prompt one tip at a time.
- Observe your child having conversations with others (sales clerks, family members, or friends). Later discuss something you noticed that they did really well. Catch them using the strategies they are learning in PEERspective.

- Encourage/insist that your child attends any and all activities PEERspective takes part in! This is essential to creating memories through shared experiences, which results in friendships.

Thank you for supporting PEERspective! By using the same vocabulary and reinforcing what is taught, you will help your child generalize these skills much more effectively. Please don't hesitate to contact me at the above email if I can support you or your child in any way!

UNIT 2

"WHERE DO THESE RULES COME FROM?"
Anticipated Middle School Behaviors

More and more educators are finding a need to intentionally teach social skills, including the ever illusive "unwritten social rules." These are the rules that really confuse our students with autism because no one has ever told them that these things need to be done, but somehow everyone else knows what to do. No wonder our friends with autism find the social world so confusing! I mean, just because a teacher stares at me, it doesn't necessarily mean that she wants me to be quiet, does it? If someone asks me a question, how do I know if they want an honest answer? Should I really tell them their new haircut looks nice when it is awful?

When you start teaching students social skills, it quickly becomes evident that so many social rules are just assumed and never taught. For example, when you were in middle or high school, how did you know where to sit at lunch? There was no sign that said "Athlete Section Only," yet there was most definitely a designated area where most of the student athletes sat, and it seemed forbidden for anyone else to sit there without an invitation. Our students do not easily pick up on these subtle nuances, which can cause major problems in all sorts of social situations.

Mindy was a sweet young lady who always went above and beyond as a peer coach. One day she asked Aspen if he would like to go see a movie with her over the weekend. His response was a very loud, "No, I don't want a girlfriend because I am not ready to make out!" Aspen did not understand that just because a girl asked him to do something outside of school, that did not mean she wanted to be his girlfriend. The bulk of Aspen's knowledge about socializing and relationships was obtained through the Disney Channel, so it makes sense that he did not understand Mindy's innocent intentions and consequently caused the young lady to be embarrassed.

While it is impossible to teach all of the expected middle school norms in one unit, what can be done is to open the students' eyes to the social world around them. By teaching some of these "rules," students start to learn that not all rules are posted and stereotypes are not fair or reliable—and that the Disney Channel programs are far from accurate.

Specific lessons include:

- Uncovering Secret Social Rules
- Interpreting Rules and Directions
- Interpreting Rules and Directions: Big Picture
- Above and Below the Line
- Thoughts and Feelings

Unit 2: Anticipated Middle School Behaviors
Lesson 1: Uncovering Secret Social Rules

LESSON OBJECTIVES

1. When watching the video clips, students will observe and identify the "Secret Social Rules" and record the rules they observe in their journals.
2. Students will take part in group and whole-class discussions about the social rules in their own school setting.
3. Students will collaborate to create and present a "Secret Social Rules" visual with their class.

RATIONALE

This lesson is used to help students understand the secret social rules in different school settings. Providing visuals of someone else's behavior is usually much easier than recognizing it on our own. Due to a lack of social awareness, many students on the spectrum have difficulty knowing if their behavior is inappropriate (Iovannone, Dunlap, & Kincaid, 2003). This lesson is a good way to provide parameters in different unstructured settings that many students may struggle with.

LESSON OVERVIEW AND INSTRUCTION

Lesson Duration

Two or three 45-minute periods

Lesson Materials

- Document platform such as Google Docs, Word, etc.
- YouTube clips
- Writing utensils

Lesson Activity

1. Students are placed in groups of 3 to 5, combining peer coaches and targeted students.
2. Students are shown video clips of "Secret Social Rules" via YouTube. https://www.youtube.com/playlist?list=PLGIcqu5UUAb1YserLQ-AL6uTZC-H4WDZF

3. Students discuss the question, "By observing others, how do you know what the social expectation is?"
4. Groups are assigned a school setting (e.g., classroom, hallway, cafeteria, recess, bathroom, library, school dance, sporting event, etc.). They will then work together to determine the most important social rules for their assigned school setting.
5. After determining the social rules for their setting, groups create a visual about the social rules of their setting to be displayed in the classroom.
6. Finally, groups present their rules and visuals to the class.

Social Emotional Learning Competencies (CASEL, 2020) addressed in this lesson:

- Self-Awareness
- Self-Management
- Responsible Decision-Making
- Social Awareness

Uncovering Secret Social Rules

Name_____ Date_____

Assigned Area: _____

Group Members: _____

Once you have been assigned your specific area from school, work with your group to decide what the most important secret social rules are for that area. After you decide on those rules, create your own document to type up the rules with your group. You can use this page as a brainstorming spot. You can decide how you'd like to decorate your document and add pictures. After you have created your document, be ready to share your rules and design with the class!

Secret social rules in this area are:

1.
2.
3.
4.
5.
6.
7.
8.
9.
10.

Unit 2: Anticipated Middle School Behaviors
Lesson 2: Interpreting Rules and Directions

LESSON OBJECTIVES

1. Students will complete the specific task without being given written or verbal instructions.
2. Students will use their knowledge of social situations to interpret what would be the socially appropriate action to take based on peers' behaviors.

RATIONALE

Social awareness is an important skill for students to develop. In real life, students will be faced with certain situations where they may not know what to do. In order to act in a socially appropriate manner, it is a good idea to look around and see what others are doing and to follow. This way, their peers will not single them out for being unsure of what to do.

LESSON OVERVIEW AND INSTRUCTION

Lesson Duration

One 45-minute period

Lesson Materials

- Construction paper
- Scissors
- Tape
- Any other materials for your task of choice

Lesson Activity

1. The teacher will begin the class period without speaking. While this lesson can be completed with any task, our suggestion is cutting out stars to create a collage. The teacher will have the supplies for the lesson laid out on a table. They can have preassembled boxes of supplies for the students, or have the students gather their own supplies.
2. Without any verbal prompting or instruction, the teacher should model the task that should be completed.

3. Students will then start to understand the directions and begin completing the task on their own.
4. At the end of the activity, the teacher should ask some reflective questions. Some of these questions may include, How did you figure out what you were supposed to do? How did watching your peers affect your understanding of the directions? and What can this apply to in the real world?

Social Emotional Learning Competencies (CASEL, 2020) addressed in this lesson:

- Self-Awareness
- Self-Management
- Responsible Decision-Making
- Social Awareness

Unit 2: Anticipated Middle School Behaviors
Lesson 3: Interpreting Rules and Directions—Big Picture

LESSON OBJECTIVES

1. Students will complete the specific task without being given written or verbal instructions.
2. Students will use their knowledge of social situations to interpret what would be the socially appropriate action to take based on peers' behaviors.

RATIONALE

Like the previous lesson, this lesson highlights social awareness in school settings. It will showcase to the school community that using peers and others around you to decide your behavior can be extremely beneficial when you are not sure what the socially appropriate behavior would be.

LESSON OVERVIEW AND INSTRUCTION

Lesson Duration

One 45-minute period

Lesson Materials

- Construction paper
- Scissors
- Tape
- Any other materials for your task of choice

Lesson Activity

1. Once the students have completed the lesson in their individual classes, the lesson can then be brought to the entire school; the students in your class can help set up a table in the hallway with cut-out shapes of your choice. At the table, there will be the necessary supplies, but no directions.
2. Students are challenged with demonstrating to their peers what should be done. The intent is to have each student that passes by look at what their peers have done and then choose

to add to the artwork on the wall. This ripple effect of adding to the wall will demonstrate to the entire school the lesson of watching your peers to figure out the socially appropriate behavior.

Social Emotional Learning Competencies (CASEL, 2020) addressed in this lesson:

- Self-Awareness
- Self-Management
- Responsible Decision-Making
- Social Awareness

Unit 2: Anticipated Middle School Behaviors
Lesson 4: Above andBelow the Line

LESSON OBJECTIVES

1. Students will listen and understand the concept of *Above the Line* and *Below the Line* behavior/actions.
2. Students will work in small groups to brainstorm and write examples of these behaviors.
3. Students will effectively communicate to their groups the thoughts, ideas, and opinions that they would like to contribute.
4. Students will share their group's ideas with the class and hang them on the wall.

RATIONALE

During PEERspective, one of the most important concepts we teach is to control your thoughts and feelings and to think socially. This activity allows the students to have ownership of the rules and expectations during class, in groups and in other settings around the school. The concept of *Above the Line* and *Below the Line* helps students see behavior not as "good or bad" but as a choice that will cause others to have thoughts and feelings about you. The visual display in the classroom is a concrete example and reminder throughout the year that can serve as a life rule in the future.

LESSON OVERVIEW AND INSTRUCTION

Lesson Duration

Two 45-minute periods

Lesson Materials

- Note cards
- Markers
- Area in the classroom to display note cards created during lesson
- Handout: two signs—*Above the Line, Below the Line* (included in the drive)

Lesson Activity

1. The students are divided into small groups of four to five (peers and targeted students intentionally grouped together).
2. On day one, present the idea of actions or behaviors being "Above or Below the Line" (People Leaders, 2019). *Above the Line* behavior is open, accepting, and curious, whereas *Below the Line* behavior is closed-minded, abrupt, blames others, and does not take responsibility. Associate these actions with behavior in the classroom (blurting out answers, rude comments, being late to class), as well as group/partner work rules (listening to other group members' comments, keeping things in your thought bubble, etc.)
3. On day two, each group is to create some *Above and Below the Line* rules and examples on note cards that will be shared with the class. It is suggested that you have each group share and put their cards on the board, and then choose which ones you'll display for the year from this brainstorm.
4. At the end of the second day, you should have a visual representation of what the expectations are for the class, based on this concept and their input. You can revisit this visual when you need to redirect behavior or as a review before group or partner work. You can also add things to this visual throughout the year, based on the needs of your classroom/students.

Social Emotional Learning Competencies (CASEL, 2020) addressed in this lesson:

- Self-Awareness
- Self-Management
- Responsible Decision-Making
- Relationship Skills
- Social Awareness

Above the Line

(open, accepting, kind, and curious)

| Listen to others' thoughts and opinions | Keep unkind thoughts in your thought bubble | Complete and submit your assignments on time |

Below the Line

(closed-minded, abrupt, blames others, not kind)

| Blurting out answers and comments | Making rude comments | Being late to class (without pass) |

This is just an example. Change the cards however necessary to meet your individual needs.

Unit 2: Anticipated Middle School Behaviors
Lesson 5: Thoughts and Feelings

LESSON OBJECTIVES

1. Students will review the concept of *Above the Line* and *Below the Line* behavior/actions.
2. Students will complete a journal about how *Above and Below the Line* behaviors make them feel.
3. Students will work in small groups to share their journals and then brainstorm and write down on the note cards how others may feel, based on their behavior.
4. Students will effectively communicate to their groups the thoughts, ideas, and opinions that they would like to contribute.

RATIONALE

During PEERspective, one of the most important concepts we teach is to control your thoughts and feelings and to think using the social mind frame. This activity takes the previous lesson to the next level by connecting behavior to how others think and feel about you. The concept of *Above the Line* and *Below the Line* helps students see behavior not as "good or bad" but as a choice that will cause others to have thoughts and feelings about them. The visual display in the classroom is a concrete example and reminder throughout the year and can serve as a life rule in the future. Students often miss the fact that what they say and do has a lasting impact on those around them and consequently on their future relationships both at school and at work.

LESSON OVERVIEW AND INSTRUCTION

Lesson Duration

One to two 45-minute periods

Lesson Materials

- Area in the classroom to display the thought bubble handout
- Note cards
- Writing utensils
- Student journals
- Handout: Thoughts and Feelings

Lesson Activity

1. This lesson starts with a quick review of "Above or Below the Line" (People Leaders, 2019). *Above the Line* behavior is open, accepting, and curious, whereas *Below the Line* behavior is closed-minded, abrupt, blames others, and does not take responsibility. As mentioned in the previous lesson, be sure to associate these actions with behavior in the classroom (blurting answers, rude comments, being late to class), as well as group/partner work rules (listening to other group members' comments, keeping thoughts in your thought bubble, etc.).
2. After reviewing this concept and referring to the display of student-created note cards in the classroom, have the students take out their journals and answer the following prompt: When people around me do *Above the Line* behaviors, it makes me feel_____because_____. Then have them do the same journal with *Below the Line* behaviors.
3. In small groups, have the students discuss what they wrote in their journals.
4. Then give each group two note cards and ask them to write down feelings associated with the named *Above the Line* behavior and *Below the Line* behavior. Be sure to connect that the actions and feelings of others cause us to have thoughts and feelings about them.
5. Then use the provided handout or a blank thought bubble template to add the thoughts and feelings others could have based on both Ab*ove and Below the Line* behaviors. You can revisit or add to this visual when you need to redirect behavior or as a reminder throughout the year.

This lesson can be done in one class period or, based on the amount of time spent in discussion and group work, could lead to a two-day lesson. Throughout the school year, be sure to refer to this display often. Remind students that others are having thoughts and feelings about them all day long and they are in charge of their own behaviors, which can then cause people to have positive or negative feelings with their daily interactions.

Social Emotional Learning Competencies (CASEL, 2020) addressed in this lesson:

- Self-Awareness
- Self-Management
- Responsible Decision-Making
- Relationship Skills
- Social Awareness

UNIT 2: "WHERE DO THESE RULES COME FROM?"   69

Above the Line = Others have <u>good thoughts</u> about you!

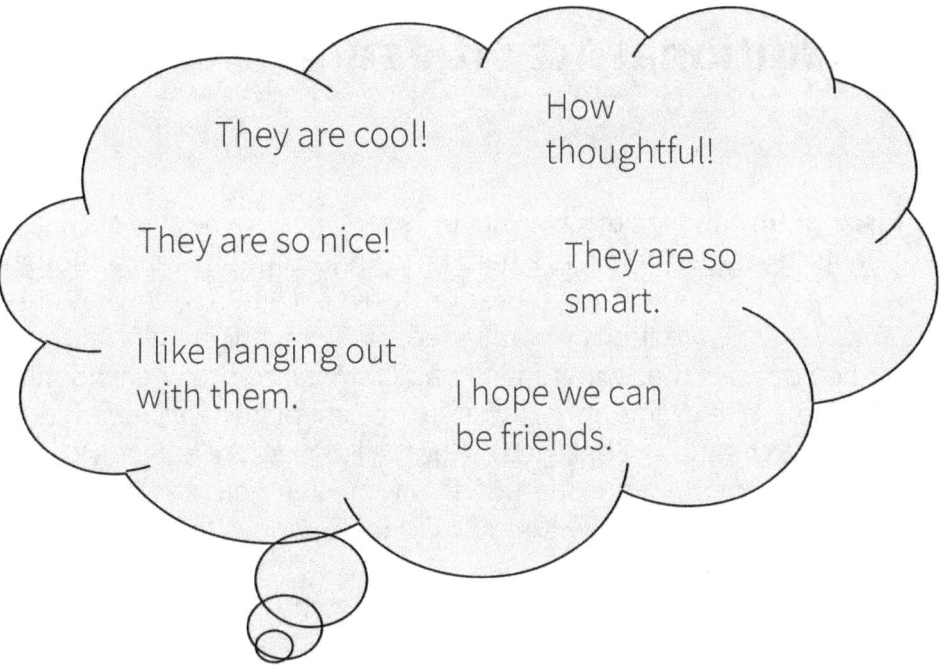

Below the Line = Others could have <u>negative thoughts</u> about you!

*This is just an example; change the comments to meet your individual needs.

Unit 2: Anticipated Middle School Behaviors Additional Activities and Ideas

- **Stereotype Discussion:** Although teaching about stereotypes can be challenging, it is necessary. I have had students in the past who had a hard time understanding that although stereotypes exist and may be based on some truth, there are always exceptions, and it is important to not judge others. Another generalization I've witnessed is when a student with autism is mistreated by a peer, and then decides that *any* student who is similar to the one who mistreated them must also be avoided. One example was when a football player was mean to the student at recess, and as a result, the student believed all football players are bullies. Having a discussion and opening the lines of communication on this topic can help students see past some of these past judgments. Here are a few examples of lesson ideas to teach this topic:

  1. Ask students to write the definition of what a stereotype is, then compare their definition to the one in the dictionary and discuss.
  2. Have students journal about what stereotypes exist in their school environment. Then create a compilation of their lists to discuss.
  3. Have students interview a parent or other adult to discuss what stereotypes existed when they were in middle or high school. Invite the students to share information from this assignment, either voluntarily or anonymously.

- **Question Box**: Decorate a box and place it in your classroom so students can anonymously ask questions. Students in your class will have very different social experiences and may feel uncomfortable (especially at the beginning of the year). Any questions in the box can be answered every Friday. You may be shocked at the social questions that come your way and the conversations that start because of these questions. Please note: Do not have students read these, as you may need to filter or paraphrase!

- **Hidden Curriculum** (Smith Myles, 2013): *The Hidden Curriculum* is a book written by Brenda Smith Myles (author of this book's foreword), and it is a tremendous resource. Brenda uncovers all of the social rules that are just observed and never explicitly taught. Students on the spectrum are often unaware of these unwritten rules, leading to confusion and uncomfortable social encounters. Using this book is a way to introduce this concept and refer back to it throughout the year.

- **Role Play:** Before any social gathering (school dances, assemblies, holidays), discuss and act out the expected behavior and unwritten social rules related to the gathering. This can lend itself to using video modeling and recording the role-play. If you have the students discuss and act out what *not* to do along with what to do, always end on what to do!

- **Conversation Challenge:** After starting conversations, the next skill is maintaining a conversation. A fun way to get the students to practice this skill is to give them a topic and set a timer. For example, the teacher can pair up students, set a timer for one minute, and say, "Talk about your weekend plans." The goal is to keep the conversation going the entire time. You could help emphasize the back and forth of a conversation by giving each pair a small ball and having them toss it to their partner when the conversation goes to their partner. This can also be a fun way to incorporate mapping and teaching conversation threads. After the students finish their minute, have them map out (draw) where the conversation started (their weekend) and where it went from there. Have you ever thought, How did we start talking about this topic? The conversation thread gradually led to the new topic through your conversation!

Teacher name:
Teacher email address:
Date:

Parent Corner
Unit 2
Anticipated Middle School Behaviors

We covered the following concepts in Unit 2:

- **Social rules change** based on your age, environment, and how well you know those around you. Look around and observe others to see what the anticipated behavior is in any given situation. (This will work throughout your whole life!)
- Behavior that is **above the line** (good choice) is open, accepting, kind, and curious. Examples are listening to others' points of view, using a thought bubble (filtering your thoughts), and being responsible by completing and submitting your assignments on time.
- Behavior that is **below the line** (not the best choice) is closed-minded, abrupt, blames others, and unkind. Examples are blurting out answers and comments, making rude comments, and being late to class (without a pass).
- People have **good, negative, or neutral thoughts** about you based on your behavior. **Stereotypes** exist, but we should try not to judge people based on how they look, what they do, or any other factors.

Next steps at home:

- When out in public or at family gatherings, prompt your child to look around at the expected behavior (figure out the social rules). An example would be at a family gathering where the appetizers are out, but no one has had any yet. The "rule" is that you are not supposed to eat them yet. You should wait for someone to announce that they are available to eat.
- Have candid and respectful discussions about stereotypes when the opportunity arises. Sometimes this can happen during a TV show you are watching; it doesn't have to be an actual, real-life situation.
- Point out when your child's behavior is "above the line" or "below the line." For example, if they make a rude comment to a sibling, you can say, "Making rude comments and not filtering your thoughts is below the line." Remind your child that others are having thoughts and feelings about them based on their words and actions.

Thank you for supporting PEERspective! By using the same vocabulary and reinforcing what is taught, you will help your child generalize these skills much more effectively. Please don't hesitate to contact me at the above email if I can support you or your child in any way!

UNIT 3

"WHAT IF THINGS DON'T GO MY WAY?"
Dealing with Setbacks and Change

Teaching students to filter their thoughts based on their audience is really all about teaching them to think socially. Let's get real: if you said everything that popped into your head, would you be employed right now? I am going to plead the fifth on that one. The point is that in order to have success and fulfillment in life, a person must learn to filter their thoughts by thinking socially.

> *All middle school students lack a filter in some ways. I remember my own daughter was known for her lack of filtering (and not in a good way) back in middle school. Her teacher asked her to pay attention one day in class and she looked right at this lovely lady and said, "I just cannot pay attention because your purple eyeshadow is really ugly, and you are not supposed to put it all the way up to your eyebrow." Now for some context, she had just had her first makeup application lesson for the upcoming show choir season, so she thought she was somewhat of an expert. However, this isn't the call you want to get as a teacher working in the district, let alone working as the social skills "expert." Elyse, like other middle school students, was often brutally honest, and students with autism are much the same.*

Along with filtering our thoughts and comments, no one likes to be told that things will not be going the way they want them to. Many of us can roll with the punches, but students with autism are often agitated by change and setbacks (Gillott et al., 2001). Resiliency is among the most important character traits we can teach our next generation and is one of the predictors of success in life (Yeager & Dweck, 2012).

Specific lessons include:

- My Mantra
- Calming Plan
- Being Mentally Flexible: Comic Strip Project
- Bouncing Back
- Problem-Solving Regulator

Unit 3: Dealing with Setbacks and Change
Lesson 1: My Mantra

LESSON OBJECTIVES

1. Students will learn about mantras that they can use to adjust their mindset.
2. Students will create or choose their own positive, inspiring, or encouraging mantra.

RATIONALE

Personal mantras are affirmative statements that students can use to help them adjust their frame of mind when they are struggling behaviorally, socially, or personally. Creating their own mantra makes the saying personal and meaningful to them. Teachers can use these mantras to help students adjust their mindset when they are struggling to minimize reactions and get back on track. It also helps if a teacher redirects or prompts a student who is struggling by using a mantra that is personal to them (i.e., the other students are unaware of its purpose). This is critical for successful interactions and interventions with students at the middle school level who are more socially aware of their differences among their peers.

LESSON OVERVIEW AND INSTRUCTION

Lesson Duration

One 45-minute class period

Lesson Materials

- My Mantra poster page
- Journals
- Colored pencils, crayons, markers, etc.
- Pencil

Lesson Activity

1. Students will begin with a journal entry where they will brainstorm ideas for their mantras by answering the following questions:
2. What motivates or encourages you when you feel negative thoughts?

3. Do you believe that what you say to yourself matters?
4. What quotes or symbols inspire you?
5. What is a personal mantra?
6. What would your personal mantra be?
7. After students have completed their journal entries with the questions above, provide time for students to share their ideas and collaborate on some symbols to represent their ideas.
8. After sharing ideas, pass out the My Mantra poster page for each student to complete. They should include their final mantra (saying, quote, etc.) on this page as well as a visual to represent their mantra. These should be colored.
9. Students can share their final mantras, and the teacher can post them in the classroom to remind students of their mantra if they are having negative thoughts or a bad day.

Social Emotional Learning Competencies (CASEL, 2020) addressed in this lesson:

- Self-Awareness
- Self-Management

Student example of the My Mantra activity by student Ricky

UNIT 3: "WHAT IF THINGS DON'T GO MY WAY?" 77

My Mantra

Use the bubble below to share the mantra or saying that you're going to live by this year. You should draw an accompanying picture or decorate using color and your imagination!

Name_____ Date_____

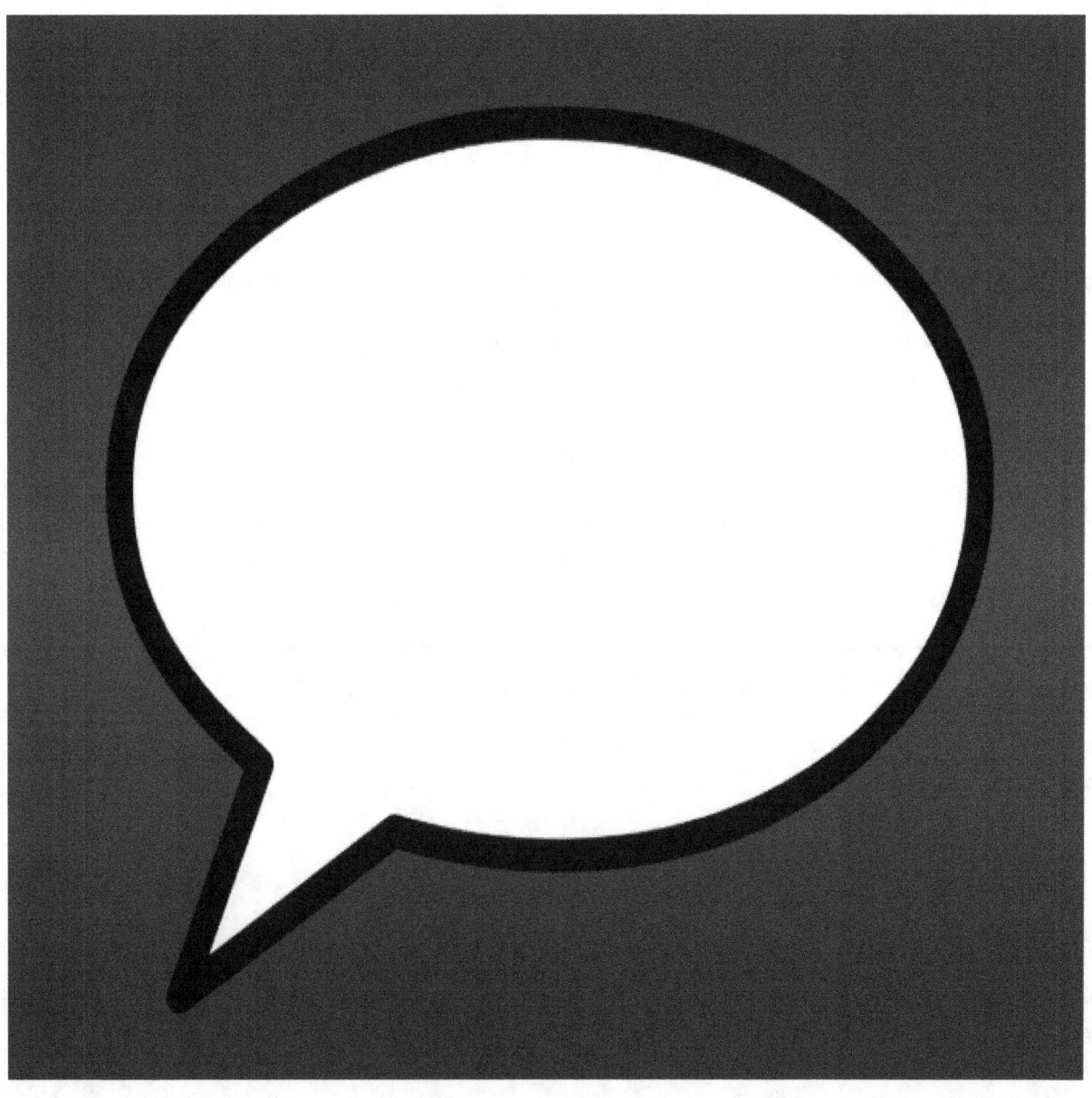

My Mantra Is

Unit 3: Dealing with Setbacks and Change
Lesson 2: Calming Plan

LESSON OBJECTIVES

1. Students will work to identify what they feel when they are not calm.
2. Students will learn a variety of calming strategies to use when feeling escalated.
3. Students will create a document that details a calming plan to share with parents and teachers to ensure everyone involved is aware of their plan and able to help implement these strategies when they feel overwhelmed, anxious, or upset in a given situation.

RATIONALE

In this lesson, students will try a variety of calming strategies to assist with self-regulation. The lesson provides students an opportunity to understand what their body feels like when they are escalated and struggling to control their emotions. They will identify the bad and good choices associated with these feelings and brainstorm strategies to help them get back to a place where their emotions are under control and they're ready to learn. A written plan makes this concept more concrete for students, and sharing the plan with parents and teachers helps the students advocate for what they need to get on track with their emotions when stressed or overwhelmed. It also helps parents and teachers by keeping them informed and involved in the team decision-making process for what is most helpful for a specific targeted student.

LESSON OVERVIEW AND INSTRUCTION

Lesson Duration

One or two 45-minute class periods

Lesson Materials

- Google Docs or other shared document platform for collaboration
- Calming Strategies Testing handout
- My Calming Plan template
- Pencil

Lesson Activity

1. Students will begin by identifying physical behaviors that indicate they are escalating and write these in the My Calming Plan document. They will complete the rest of this handout after testing some calming strategies.
2. The teacher and/or occupational therapist, if available, will explain and demonstrate calming strategies to use when students feel like they are struggling to control their emotions.
3. Students will try various strategies presented to them by the teacher and/or occupational therapist.
4. As students attempt each strategy, they will write down what they feel when they attempt these strategies on the Calming Strategies Testing handout provided.
5. Once students have identified their preferred calming strategies, they will develop a five-step calming strategy, and they will input their strategies on the provided template.
6. After completing their calming strategies plan, students will review it with partners and the teacher. They will then print it to take home and share with their parents. They will bring it back signed, acknowledging that their parents have reviewed the plan with their child.

Social Emotional Learning Competencies (CASEL, 2020) addressed in this lesson:

- Self-Awareness
- Self-Management

Students enjoy testing out a claiming strategy: yoga as a whole class.

Sample Calming Strategies Testing

As you try each station, write a brief description of what you did next to the title and whether you think it would be helpful to use when you feel frustrated, overwhelmed, or anxious.

Name_____ Date_____

Station 1: Weighted blanket	My Thoughts:
Station 2: Calming scents (including lavender, vanilla, banana, and coconut), with student controlling placement and amount of smell	
Station 3: Putty or playdough	
Station 4: Crunchy or chewy snacks (carrots, licorice, beef jerky, bagel, gummy bears, etc.)	
Station 5: Squeeze a stress ball	
Station 6: Yoga poses	
Station 7: Wall push-ups	
Station 8: Pressing hands together	
Station 9: Blowing bubbles	
Station 9: Deep breathing	
Station 10: Doodling	

UNIT 3: "WHAT IF THINGS DON'T GO MY WAY?" 81

My Calming Plan

Name_____ Date_____

Physical ways I can tell I am leaving my calm feelings:

Thinking About My Options:

Bad Choices:

Good Choices:

My plan when I feel myself getting overwhelmed, frustrated, or anxious (must have at least five steps):

Unit 3: Dealing with Setbacks and Change
Lesson 3: Being Mentally Flexible Comic Strip Project

LESSON OBJECTIVES

1. Students will utilize a rubric to create a mental flexibility visual representation.
2. Students will present/display their comic strip project in order to explain how the flexible thinking concept applies to their visual.
3. Students will work to understand the other examples of being mentally flexible provided by their peers.

RATIONALE

In this lesson, the students will work on the concept of shifting their mindset and becoming more flexible. Being mentally flexible during frustrating situations is an important life skill for everyone, but it can be especially difficult for students with autism. When things don't go the way they think they should, learning to change the way they think about a situation will empower students to deal with setbacks in a positive way. Leaning to change their mindset toward addressing adversity or difficult situations while working with a group will help PEERspective students practice necessary life skills that will help them succeed in real-life situations. The rubric provided gives students a concrete idea of the expectations and requirements in order to do well on the project. The rubric specifically identifies students' ability to be flexible and work in groups for the project, and also focuses on their presentation skills using previously discussed strategies. Students enjoy utilizing their creativity, while also working on changing their mindset when addressing adversity or difficult situations while completing this project in groups.

LESSON OVERVIEW AND INSTRUCTION

Lesson Duration

One or two 45-minute periods

Lesson Materials

- Student journal for drafting ideas
- Pen, pencil, coloring materials
- Comic strip template

Lesson Activity

1. The class will brainstorm social setbacks that they have experienced or seen play out in real life or on a TV show (for example, not getting the grade wanted on a test, having a disagreement with a friend, not eating the meal you wanted for dinner, forgetting to complete your homework for the next day).
2. Students will be grouped and assigned a social setback to illustrate via a comic strip presentation. Groups will create a visual representation of being mentally flexible in frustrating situations that don't go the way they think they should. Groups are given two options:
3. Make all three lines (nine boxes) of the comic strip template into one large comic showing how to think in a more flexible way about their given scenario.
4. Show three separate examples of being flexible/adapting to change, using one line (three boxes) for each example.
5. Students then present their comic strips or display them to the class to explain how they represent the idea of being mentally flexible and adaptive to social setbacks.

Social Emotional Learning Competencies (CASEL, 2020) addressed in this lesson:

- Responsible Decision-Making
- Relationship Skills
- Social Awareness

Being Mentally Flexible: Comic Strip Project

Name_____ Date_____

Requirements:

- Each comic strip needs to include dialogue (word bubbles) and narration (square narration boxes).

- You have two options that your group needs to decide on as a whole for completing this project:

    a. Make all three lines of the comic strip template (nine boxes) one large comic showing mental flexibility.
    b. Make three separate examples of mental flexibility (three boxes for each example).

- Please show your best effort. It is okay if you are not the best artist, as long as you create good examples and work in your group to try your best!

www.PrintablePaper.net

Grading Rubric:

	4	3	2	1
Knowledge: Using an understanding of what mental flexibility is and demonstrating it in the comic.	Students showed a complete understanding of what mental flexibility is and provided strong example(s).	Students had only minor issues or mistakes with providing example(s) of mental flexibility.	Students had 3 or more issues with providing example(s) for being mentally flexible.	Students clearly do not understand what mental flexibility is or how to demonstrate it.
Completion: Students have a complete comic strip with one large example or 3 small examples of mental flexibility with dialogue and narration.	Students completed all requirements for the comic project.	Students completed a majority of the requirements for the comic project.	Students completed some of the requirements for the comic project.	Students did not complete the project or barely completed requirements for the comic project.
Group Work: Students worked effectively in their groups and used strategies associated with mental flexibility.	Students exceeded expectations in their effort to work in groups for this project.	Students applied a great amount of effort into working in groups.	Students did some good group work on this project but could have worked more collaboratively.	Students applied very little effort into working in groups for this project.
Quality: Students attempted a good story with pictures and color.	Students produced high-quality work on this project from beginning to end.	Students produced a project that is good quality.	Students started out strong but rushed to finish in the end.	Project has many mistakes and is messy.

Group Member Names: _____

Score: _____ / _____ points

Unit 3: Dealing with Setbacks and Change
Lesson 4: Bouncing Back

LESSON OBJECTIVES

1. Students will learn about the concept of bouncing back from a frustrating event using the visual representation of an egg and a bouncy ball.
2. Students will use the visual representation of mental flexibility and relate the concept to their current situations when they feel frustrated or face a problem.
3. Students will share their responses to the activity with their peers and participate in a class discussion.

RATIONALE

This lesson is an interactive and engaging lesson that students thoroughly enjoy. Its purpose is to help students visualize the concept of "bouncing back" when they've had a setback in the various settings of their lives. This lesson uses the visual of an egg, which breaks, and a bouncy ball, which bounces back. When students can visualize the concept of bouncing back when they are not personally in a frustrating moment, they are better able to see the reactions for themselves and later utilize these visuals to respond more appropriately in various situations. Students also really enjoy this activity because of the activeness of it and because—let's face it—they are middle schoolers and they get to throw things. The physical action allows them to connect more meaningfully to the journal entry and creates more productive conversations and reactions among their peers. The sharing process also shows students that they are not the only ones who may have negative reactions when frustrated. The shared experience makes them more likely to share openly and to use those positive interactions and strategies when they are frustrated in authentic settings.

UNIT 3: "WHAT IF THINGS DON'T GO MY WAY?"

LESSON OVERVIEW AND INSTRUCTION

Lesson Duration

One 45-minute period

Lesson Materials

- Eggs (1 per student)
- Bouncy balls (1 per student)
- Standing target
- Tarp or protective covering
- Student Journal
- Pen/pencil

Lesson Activity

1. This lesson is best completed outside, as it can get a little messy. You should also ensure your administration is aware and approves of the lesson! (Never hurts to inform your custodians as well!) After approval, set up a large target.
2. Students line up and take turns throwing the egg at the target. The target represents their personal problem or setback. When they throw the egg, they will notice the hard shell cracks and is destroyed on impact.
3. In the next round, students take turns throwing a bouncy ball at the target. They will notice that the bouncy ball is flexible and resilient and bounces back from the target.
4. Once each student has completed the process for both the egg and the bouncy ball, students turn to their journals and answer the following questions relating to the activity:
5. Does the hard-shelled egg represent mental flexibility or not? What does it represent?
6. How does the bouncy ball represent mental flexibility?
7. Which of the two examples is better when you are faced with a setback or problem in your life?
8. Can you think of an example when you have had to use flexible thinking (like the ball?) or a moment when you were hard-headed (like the egg) and could have used flexible thinking? Explain.

After students have answered the questions in their journal, share responses as a whole group. This also creates a class discussion about shared experiences.

Social Emotional Learning Competencies (CASEL, 2020) addressed in this lesson:

- Self-Awareness
- Self-Management

Students enjoy the visual exercise of bouncing back to setbacks by throwing eggs and balls outside.

Unit 3: Dealing with Setbacks and Change
Lesson 5: Problem-Solving Regulator

LESSON OBJECTIVES

1. Students will identify different problems that they may encounter and determine the appropriate reaction to match the situation.
2. Students will interact and share information with their peers in a conversational manner to discuss problems and reactions.
3. Students will create their own regulator visual to represent the problems they come up with and what their reactions would be for each situation.

RATIONALE

In this lesson, students will work together in groups to identify different problems they may encounter in their middle school lives. While determining these problems, they will discuss where these problems would fall in terms of severity. Determining the severity of each problem is an essential piece to regulating their emotions and reactions and facilitating their independence in solving their everyday problems. Students' regulators are used to help them gauge whether or not the situation matches how upset they feel and whether their reactions are appropriate for the given situation.

LESSON OVERVIEW AND INSTRUCTION

Lesson Duration

One 45-minute class period

Lesson Materials

- Journals
- Large poster board
- Coloring utensils

Lesson Activity

1. Group students to identify problems and reactions; as a group, they are to ensure that both concepts match. By making this a group project, students must discuss their decisions and give concrete examples to show one another why a specific reaction matches what their problem is.
2. Groups also create a visual representation to allow other students to better understand how their problem and their reaction should match on their regulator.
3. Students can then share their different examples, because many students probably have encountered similar situations in their middle school lives.
4. If necessary, you can also provide examples to each group that they can discuss and create visual representations for. It is best to provide examples for low reaction, medium reaction, and big reaction problems, so that students can appropriately gauge the differences in the reactions. Examples of some possible problems students could use to brainstorm solutions and reactions for this lesson include:

    o I forgot to complete my homework last night.
    o My parents decided we would eat my least favorite meal for dinner.
    o My best friend told my other friend about the mean comment I made about their hair.
    o I left my textbook at school, which has all of the problems I need to finish for homework tonight.
    o I didn't charge my Chromebook last night and now I'm going to have a consequence at school.
    o I fell asleep during class and my teacher emailed home and told my parents.
    o I lied to my parents about how I got a bad grade on my science test.
    o My friend told me she doesn't want to play my favorite game at recess, basketball.
    o I brought my brother's lunch to school instead of my lunch.

5. These visuals can also be posted throughout the room for the class to reference at different times throughout the school year.

Social Emotional Learning Competencies (CASEL, 2020) addressed in this lesson:

- Self-Awareness
- Self-Management
- Responsible Decision-Making
- Social Awareness

Unit 3: Dealing with Setbacks and Change
Additional Activities and Ideas

- **Change Ahead:** Schedule changes at middle schools happen, so it's helpful to have a structured way to share that information with your students with as much advance notice as possible. Simply having a visual "change ahead" sign to put on the board and writing down any upcoming changes can help your students have a much better day.

- **Problem-Solving Center:** Consider having an area in your classroom that is the "Problem-Solving Center." Make it a calm environment well stocked with supplies (paper, pens, etc.) where students can think about how to handle something that hasn't gone well in their day. If a student has trouble asking for time to de-escalate, you may want to consider a way for the student to let you know that they need your help problem-solving (like a break card).

- **Visual Cues:** Many of our social communication students are in general education or advanced classes throughout their day. One way to help them stay on task and remember to filter their thoughts is by using visual cues. Comment cards can remind the students to filter their thoughts by making no more than three comments or questions each class period. This boundary can help the student become more selective about what they share or ask during a class period. If they have questions after they use their three comment cards, they can ask.

- **Worrying Template/Journal Prompt:** Journaling as a coping mechanism is a useful tool for our students with autism. Inspired by a podcast episode titled "Back to School Panic" from *Losing 100 Pounds with Corinne* by Corinne Crabtree (2020), the template found at the end of this unit allows students to get their worries and emotions on paper and then decide whether they can or can't control them. If they can control them, then the student creates an action plan to do so; if they cannot control them, they need to let the worry go and use a calming strategy (Unit 3, Lesson 2), such as a mantra (Unit 3, Lesson 1).

My Worry Journal Name: _____

Below each box, answer the journal prompt and "dump" all of your worries and associated thoughts and feelings in the space provided. Remember, feelings are not wrong or right: they just are feelings. This is a safe place to get worries out of your mind and create a plan to deal with them. (Crabtree, 2020)

Write your worries here.	How does this worry make you feel?	Is this worry a **Can** or **Can't** control for you?	If you **Can** control it, what will you do about it, starting right now?	If you **Can't** control it, what calming strategy will you use to overcome this thought?

Teacher name:
Teacher email address:
Date:

Parent Corner
Unit 3
Dealing with Setbacks and Change

We covered the following concepts in Unit 3:

- **Personal mantras** are affirmative statements that students can use to help them adjust their frame of mind when struggling behaviorally, socially, or personally.
- "For many of us, controlling our emotions and body comes fairly naturally. For others, this is not the case. Those with regulation difficulties lack this innate ability to think through and succeed in everyday stressful situations. For them, **emotional control and self-regulation must be learned and practiced**" (Kuypers & Winner, 2019).
- Examples of **self-regulation and calming strategies** include weighted blanket, calming scents, crunchy or chewy snacks (e.g., carrots, licorice, beef jerky, bagel, gummy bears, etc.), squeezing a stress ball, yoga poses.
- Having a bad moment doesn't mean you have to have a bad day. Learning to "**bounce back**" and "not splat" was a theme in this unit that the students will continue to hear throughout the school year.
- When dealing with problems, our reactions should be similar in size to the situation. We discussed low, medium, and big reaction situations and discussed how we can **try to regulate our emotions so that our reaction matches the situation**.

Next steps at home:

- Ask your child what their mantra is.
- When you observe your child starting to escalate, or when they are faced with a difficult situation, remind your child to use their mantra (or recite their mantra to them).
- Discuss with your child what calming strategies you use for yourself and what strategies they find helpful when feeling escalated. Be intentional about discussing that it's okay if you use different strategies.
- If you notice your student escalating in a way that is not proportionate to the situation, encourage them to use their problem-solving regulator skills to match their reactions to the situation.

Thank you for supporting PEERspective! By using the same vocabulary and reinforcing what is being taught, you will help your child generalize these skills much more effectively. Please don't hesitate to contact me at the above email if I can support you or your child in any way!

UNIT 4

"HOW DO I KEEP IT ALL STRAIGHT?"
Executive Functioning

In a recent discussion with my daughter, a college freshman, I told her that the most important skill for success in college is time management. I then took a deep breath and realized what I had said and the implications that would have on my students, or as I like to call them, my "school children." Time management is one of the essential executive functioning skills that take place in the frontal lobe and are responsible for helping you to get things done. "Just as an air traffic control system at a busy airport safely manages the arrivals and departures of many aircraft on multiple runways, the brain needs [executive functioning] to filter distractions, prioritize tasks, set and achieve goals, and control impulse" (Center on the Developing Child at Harvard University, 2015).

Executive function helps people to do many things, such as:

- Manage time
- Pay attention
- Switch focus
- Plan and organize
- Remember details
- Avoid saying or doing the wrong thing
- Do things based on experience
- Multitask

I don't know about you, but looking at the list above, many past students pop into my mind as struggling with these skills—from the super smart student who always did their homework but forgot to turn it in, to the well-intentioned student whose papers and folders covered a whole table. While not all students have deficits in all of the above-mentioned areas, it is clear that many are impacted by executive functioning deficits.

> *Before Kyle used the My Homework App, he got his assignments and worked on them and sometimes turned them in, but many times he did not. The changes in follow-through for Kyle have been wonderful because he is now getting credit for work he was completing and just not turning in. The app encourages him to complete the tasks instead of just answering questions on paper or online, and since he is rule-driven, his grades have improved! As a parent, checking the online grade book is no longer the source of anxiety it once was since he has embraced utilizing this tool.*
>
> —Beth, parent

> *I feel that My Homework has helped me learn to prioritize my assignments and get them turned in on time. My Homework is my administrative assistant because it sends me reminders to complete and turn in my assignments!*
>
> —Kyle, student

Flexibility, leveled emotionality, impulse control, planning/organizing, and problem-solving are some of the mental processes involved in executive functioning (Wilkins, S., & Burmeister, C, 2015). The following lessons will assist students in finding their strengths and weaknesses in executive functioning in order to intentionally improve these vital life skills. Obviously, teaching executive functioning is a year-long—actually, lifelong—process, but these activities will introduce the topic and create a foundation for continued work throughout the school year and beyond.

Specific lessons include:

- Executive Functioning Research Jigsaw
- Organizational Time Crunch Challenge
- "Make Your Bed" TED Talk
- Time Management Group Project
- Dear Teacher Letter/Email

Unit 4: Executive Functioning
Lesson 1: Jigsaw

LESSON OBJECTIVES

1. Students will research and identify a subtopic associated with executive functioning and create an info page on that subtopic.
2. Students will present their subtopic to each other in a jigsaw format, to send and receive information on the subtopics of executive functioning.
3. Students will work to have a basic understanding of the subtopics of executive functioning and their meaning.

RATIONALE

Executive functioning is a topic that is widely discussed but difficult for students at the middle school level to grasp. This lesson provides students an introductory understanding of all of the topics associated with executive functioning. It's important for them to understand that executive functioning is not simply organization; rather, it encompasses many different skills. Students will learn in depth about a specific subtopic, then share that knowledge with their classmates. The sharing and receiving of information among classmates provides an opportunity for students to take ownership of their work and to better retain the information. The use of the "jigsaw format to teach reading comprehension makes students more active during the teaching and learning process, and it improves their comprehension" (Neneng & Suherdi, 2018). By starting with this lesson when teaching executive functioning, students have a better understanding throughout the unit on which aspect of executive functioning is being emphasized, which improves their understanding overall.

LESSON OVERVIEW AND INSTRUCTION

Lesson Duration

Two 45-minute periods

Lesson Materials

- Student journals
- Paper
- Writing utensil
- Executive Functioning blank Google Slide template, accessible via drive
- Executive Functioning Google Slides, accessible via drive

Lesson Activity

1. In this lesson, students use the information slides and work in groups to identify and explain the basic topics associated with executive functioning. These topics include flexibility, working memory, planning/organizing, impulse control, problem-solving, sustained attention, and leveled emotionality.
2. Each group is assigned one subtopic and creates a brief information page on their subtopic via provided templates in Google Slides.
3. After creating this info page, students will break out into new groups and share information on their subtopic with other classmates. This creates the jigsaw format, where students share information on their subtopic and receive information on the other subtopics that explain executive functioning.

Social Emotional Learning Competencies (CASEL, 2020) addressed in this lesson:

- Self-Awareness
- Self-Management
- Responsible Decision-Making
- Social Awareness

Unit 4: Executive Functioning
Lesson 2: Organizational Time Crunch Challenge

LESSON OBJECTIVES

1. Students will work in groups to identify the best way to execute the activities.
2. Students will implement the tasks in the determined order, then identify what was successful and how they could have improved.

RATIONALE

In this project, groups of students put executive functioning skills to the test as they complete short, timed, "minute to win it" style tasks. As students work together on these activities, they practice various executive function strategies such as: managing time, paying attention, switching focus, planning and organizing and remembering details. The more often that students utilize these skills, the more successful they will become because the skills will happen more naturally. By creating games and fun group challenges, the students are working on generalization of these skills and building rapport with their peers at the same time.

LESSON OVERVIEW AND INSTRUCTION

Lesson Duration

One 45-minute period

Lesson Materials

- Student journals
- Writing utensils
- Time management activities
- Access to presentation template

Lesson Activity

1. Group students into teams that will work together to complete various organizational challenges (not typical school activities) listed on the challenge cards that follow this lesson. These include various fun activities that students should be able to complete as a group quickly

and easily. Each activity should be completed within a specific amount of time, and students are rewarded points for completing the activities.

Students practicing different organizational tasks in groups.

Social Emotional Learning Competencies (CASEL, 2020) addressed in this lesson:

- Self-Awareness
- Self-Management
- Responsible Decision-Making
- Social Awareness

Organizational Time Crunch Challenges

These half-sheet checklists should be utilized by each team to check off as they complete each challenge. Teacher(s) can initial after each challenge is completed.

Organizational Time Crunch Challenge

Name(s)_____ Date_____

Team Name:

Check	Teacher	
		Challenge #1: Order Up!
		Challenge #2: I have Uno!
		Challenge #3: M&M (Not the Wrapper)!
		Challenge #4: Tower of Cards!
		Challenge #5: Think Like Picasso!
		Challenge #6: One-Legged Race!
		Challenge #7: Lock it Up!

Name(s)_____ Date_____

Team Name:

Check	Teacher	
		Challenge #1: Order Up!
		Challenge #2: I have Uno!
		Challenge #3: M&M (Not the Wrapper)!
		Challenge #4: Tower of Cards!
		Challenge #5: Think Like Picasso!
		Challenge #6: One-Legged Race!
		Challenge #7: Lock it up!

Unit 4: Executive Functioning
Lesson 3: "Make Your Bed" TED Talk

LESSON OBJECTIVES

1. Students will attentively watch the video and complete the Make Your Bed TED Talk handout.
2. Students will discuss their opinions in a respectful way.
3. Students will effectively communicate to their small groups their thoughts, ideas, and opinions of the TED Talk.
4. Students will follow up on this concept independently by making their bed and/or participating in class challenges to make their bed each morning.

RATIONALE

This particular TED Talk shows that small changes in behavior can bring about changes in other areas in life. Students on the spectrum often perseverate on details, and this detail (making your bed each morning) could prove beneficial to their success in life. It is also valuable to discuss this TED Talk and see other peoples' perspectives. Learning to accept differing viewpoints can be challenging for students with autism, and exposure to ideas like this encourages them to accept differing viewpoints in a nonthreatening way. While practicing executive functioning, this lesson can show students that the planning and organizing involved in making your bed each day might have a trickle-down effect to other areas of their lives.

LESSON OVERVIEW AND INSTRUCTION

Lesson Duration

One 45-minute period

Lesson Materials

- Platform to show online video
- Handout
- Pen/pencil for each student

Lesson Activity

1. The students watch a short TED Talk found online:
   https://www.youtube.com/watch?v=3sK3wJAxGfs
   This TED Talk by Admiral William McRaven shares how the simple act of making your bed can have a ripple effect on other goals and successes throughout your day.
2. At the completion of the video, give each student the opportunity to independently complete the Make Your Bed TED Talk handout.
3. Students can discuss their answers with a small group using the discussion questions they created and then participate in a whole-class discussion.
4. At the end of the lesson, it is recommended that you debrief this lesson with "takeaways," written in the student's journal, on the board, or both.

Don't forget to revisit this idea throughout the school year. This can be done through a simple show of hands at the beginning of class asking who made their bed that morning, or a class challenge to make your bed for a set number of days in a row.

Social Emotional Learning Competencies (CASEL, 2020) addressed in this lesson:

- Self-Management
- Responsible Decision-Making
- Social Awareness

Name(s)_____ Date_____

Make Your Bed—TED Talk Discussion Questions

1. Name one reason making your bed can help you be more successful and explain why:

2. What should you do if a shark begins to circle your current position? Why do you think that is?

3. Create your own discussion questions:

    a)

    b)

Unit 4: Executive Functioning
Lesson 4: Time Management Group Project

LESSON OBJECTIVES

1. Students will work in groups to identify the best way to execute the six assigned time management tasks for the project.
2. Students will implement the tasks in the determined order, then identify what was successful and how they could have improved.
3. Students will present their successes and struggles to the class in the completion of their time management project.

RATIONALE

This culminating project has students work in groups to use the executive functioning strategies they have learned throughout the previous lessons. They will work together to implement and complete assigned tasks in their groups. Students are utilizing effective executive functioning skills while also working on flexibility in groups throughout this project. Students are encouraged to focus on impulse control and listen to their group members' ideas and opinions. Then they can work on other EF skills such as planning and organizing. Once the tasks have been completed, students will evaluate their effectiveness and success with each task and its implementation throughout the project in a brief presentation to their classmates. The sharing of their successes and struggles demonstrates to students that their classmates had similar experiences and also identifies the differences in their experiences throughout the project. Students get to work on critical presentation skills and flexibility throughout the entire project.

LESSON OVERVIEW AND INSTRUCTION

Lesson Duration

Two 45-minute periods

Lesson Materials

- Student journals
- Writing utensil
- Time management activities

- Access to a presentation template (PowerPoint, Prezi, Google Slides, etc.)
- Time management student documentation sheet, included in this lesson plan

Lesson Activity

1. Group students to complete a culminating time management project.
2. Each group receives six tasks. They must decide as a group in what order they will complete the tasks, how much time they think each one will take, and then complete them. The tasks include:

    a. Team Member Nicknames: Teams must agree on a team name and a nickname for each team member. Everyone must agree on these.
    b. Classmates' John Hancocks: Students must get a signature from every classmate in the room.
    c. Jumpin' Jack: Each team member must do at least 25 jumping jacks at some point throughout the project days.
    d. Conga Line: Teams must create a conga line from one end of the room to the other. Bonus points for getting other classmates/teachers to join in!
    e. MyTube YouTube: Teams must choose one video that shows a concept we have learned in this class. Videos should be under two minutes.
    f. Sum It Up: Each group must find an adult with whom to share three important concepts learned in class this year.

3. Students will use the documentation sheet on the next page to keep track of how and when they completed each activity. They can also use this sheet to take notes that they may use in their presentations.
4. After completing the tasks, they have to evaluate the effectiveness of their plan to complete the tasks. They will then create a presentation on their successes and lessons learned. (Students may use whatever format they would like to present: PowerPoint, Prezi, etc.)

This lesson will take two periods for students to complete the tasks and then evaluate the effectiveness of their time management. They will then briefly present the strategies they used and indicate whether or not their strategies were effective.

Social Emotional Learning Competencies (CASEL, 2020) addressed in this lesson:

- Self-Awareness
- Self-Management
- Responsible Decision-Making
- Social Awareness

Time Management Student Documentation

Group Members' Names: _____

Group Members' Nicknames: _____

Team Name: _____

Task	Documentation
Team and Member Nicknames: You must come up with a team name, and each member should have a nickname. Everyone must agree on these.	
Classmates' John Hancocks: You must get a signature from every classmate in the room.	
Jumpin' Jack: Each member from your group must do at least 25 jumping jacks at some point throughout the project days.	
Conga Line: Create a conga line from one end of the room to the other. Bonus points if you get other classmates/teachers to join in.	
MyTube YouTube: Choose one video that shows a concept that we have learned in this class. Should be no longer than 2 minutes!	
Sum It Up: Your group must find another adult (not your teacher in this class) to share 3 important concepts you have learned in SCC class this year.	

Record classmates' signatures below!

Unit 4: Executive Functioning
Lesson 5: Dear Teacher Letter/Email

LESSON OBJECTIVES

1. Students will compose a letter in proper email/letter format.
2. Students will identify pertinent background information to provide to their teacher to improve their school year.
3. Students will identify strengths and weaknesses to share with their teachers.

RATIONALE

This lesson can be utilized to help students with both leveled emotionality and planning which can open up the lines of communication with their teachers, build rapport and encourage self-advocacy. When they write this letter, they are letting their teachers know what their strengths and struggles are, as well as any pertinent personal information that may be important for the teacher to know. This helps students realize that they don't have to be good at everything, and that everyone has things they are good at and things they struggle with. They are also taking responsibility for their learning by sharing it with their other teachers. When students know what strategies work best for them in the classroom and can share those strategies—along with other relevant personal information—with their teachers, they set themselves up for a successful school year.

LESSON OVERVIEW AND INSTRUCTION

Lesson Duration

One or two 45-minute class periods

Lesson Materials

- Paper and writing utensils
  or
- Computer/email access

Lesson Activity

1. Students will be provided a sample letter that exemplifies the expected letter/email format. The letter will provide ideas of writing topics to include when composing their letter/email to their teacher.
2. Once students have brainstormed their information, including strengths and struggles, they will compose the letter to send to their teachers.

You can conduct this lesson in paper or email format, whichever is more conducive to your learning environment. If students are emailing their information to their teachers, it is advised to give teachers a heads-up about the assignment and to have students copy you on their messages. I also encourage teachers to respond to the email if they are able. The return response helps students feel valued for their efforts to provide their teachers with information that can help them succeed at school.

Social Emotional Learning Competencies (CASEL, 2020) addressed in this lesson:

- Self-Awareness
- Relationship Skills
- Social Awareness

Dear Teacher Letter or Email

Name_____ Date_____

Dear Students,

    You are extremely important to your teachers, as is your success both in and outside of school. Your teachers want to get to know the **real** you this year. The more they know about you, the better you can work together to make this year great.

    Please use the suggestions below to help your teachers get to know more about you and your strengths and struggles. The more you write, the more they will know, and the better chance you will both have a successful school year.

Sincerely,

Dear Teacher Letter or Email

Name_____ Date_____

Date

Dear Teachers,

Below are some ideas you can use for your email. Choose only what you feel most comfortable sharing with your teachers.

- **Talk about your family and yourself**
    - What makes you unique?
    - Do you have a nickname? Tell the story behind your given name or any nicknames you have acquired.
    - Tell me about your parents—names, professions, your relationship with them.
    - Tell me about your siblings—names, ages, personalities, your relationship with them.
    - Are there other family members you are close to, such as an aunt or uncle, cousins, grandparents, etc.? If so, tell me about them, too.
    - Pets? Other?

- **Strengths**
    - Tell your teachers what you are good at:
        - What subjects do you excel at and why?
        - What type of learner are you?
        - What helps you to learn?
        - What subjects are you most interested in or excited about this year?

- **Challenges**
    - Tell your teachers what you struggle with:
        - What helps you overcome those struggles or challenges?
        - What subjects are the hardest for you and why?
        - Are there any behavioral challenges or things you struggle with during class that you would like them to know? (preferred seating location, things/people that annoy or distract you)

Sincerely,

  (Sign your name here)

Unit 4: Executive Functioning
Additional Activities and Ideas

- **Puzzles:** Break up your class into groups of two or three and assign a task with a time limit. Consider having them complete a 50–100 piece puzzle in ten minutes, for example. This is also integrated into the Time Crunch Challenge lesson in this unit.

- **Game Day:** Both the high school and middle school PEERspective classes enjoy planned game days throughout the year. Consider making one of these game days focus on memory games such as name games, concentration card games, memory card games, or the tray game. All of these games require students to use their working memory and have minimal to no cost or preparation for the teacher. You can also challenge your students to pick the games and or create games to work on this skill. Below is a list of games that help students with various executive functioning skills, as found on the blog, *Pathway2Success* (Scully, 2017).

    1. Blurt!: self-control, metacognition
    2. Scrabble: planning, organizing
    3. Pictionary: flexibility, time management
    4. Distraction: working memory, attention
    5. 5 Second Rule: time management, task initiation
    6. Freeze: self-control, attention
    7. Jenga: self-control, flexibility, planning
    8. Brainteasers: perseverance, flexibility
    9. Chess: planning, flexibility, working memory
    10. Sudoku: perseverance, working memory

- **Organization Day:** Take one day each week and designate it as "organization day." Teach the students what "organized" looks like by using the checklists on the next pages with specific tasks related to organizing materials.

- **Grade Check:** Take one day each week and designate it "grade check day." Teaching students to self-monitor their grades and create a system for tracking assignments is vital. I like to use the app "myHomework." This app helps with executive functioning because it prioritizes tasks and hides the ones that are not due. It also sends emails reminding students to complete their work.

- **Checklists:** It is important to teach students that we all have strengths and weaknesses, and that the goal is not to be perfect but to create a plan for areas in our lives that don't come easy to us. When a student struggles with any skill associated with executive functioning and/or school, using tools that help them create their own checklist or visual to keep themselves on track can be empowering. For example, if a student keeps forgetting to bring home materials at the end of the day, have them create a system to fix this problem. This could be a checklist on their phone, a reminder with an alarm, or a simple checklist they print out and check off. Whatever they decide to do, they will be more motivated to succeed if it was their idea in the first place! Two sample checklists follow that you can modify and for your student's specific needs.

Sample Checklist
How to Find Success in School and Life!

Monday: Get **Organized**!

- ❏ No loose papers.
- ❏ All papers are in the right folders and sections.
- ❏ Any torn papers are reinforced.
- ❏ Any assignments that are late are turned in.

Tuesday: Grade Check Day!

- ❏ Look up your grades in each of your classes.
- ❏ Make a list of your current grades.
- ❏ Make a list of any missing assignments.
- ❏ Complete any missing assignments.
- ❏ Create a plan to complete upcoming assignments, tests, and quizzes.

Wednesday: "With it" Wednesday! Practice being **Proactive**.

- ❏ Review your list from yesterday; what grades would you like to raise?
- ❏ Review your missing assignment list and make a plan for finishing any late assignments.
- ❏ Map out any upcoming projects or long-term assignments (YES, break it into smaller pieces!)

Thursday: Test and quiz prep (this can be done on other days also!)

- ❏ Look at your teachers' websites. Are there upcoming tests and quizzes?
- ❏ Create a plan for studying for upcoming tests and quizzes (YES, break it into smaller pieces!)
- ❏ Review your notes, look over your vocabulary words, and create a "quizlet" or another game to help you study. Try https://quizlet.com/.

Friday: Friends and Family

- ❏ Think about a peer in one of your classes that you feel you could talk to, and decide what conversation-starter you'll use (e.g., Hey, what are you doing this weekend?)
- ❏ Remember that whatever you ask of someone else is usually then asked of you, too. In other words, think about *your* answer to the question you are planning to ask. (e.g., I have a soccer game, and then I'm going to my cousin's birthday party.)
- ❏ Choose at least one social event to attend with a friend or family member this weekend.

Sample Checklist
Organization 101

Name_____ Date_____

Please complete the following tasks to ensure that you are setting yourself up for success!

- ❏ I have no loose papers.
- ❏ I have cleaned out and organized my locker (no loose papers, items stacked neatly in an orderly fashion).
- ❏ I have checked my grades and recorded any missing assignments.
    - o I have contacted any teachers that I need to communicate with regarding missing work.
    - o I have created a timeline or plan to submit all missing assignments by this Sunday.
    - o I have submitted any missing assignments (preferably electronically) and emailed the teacher to let them know that I have submitted them.
    - o I have brainstormed why I had missing assignments this week and created a better plan moving forward. For example, if I didn't know there was homework, what could I do to fix that? Is there an app I could use to stay organized?

Notes/Action Items:

Teacher Comments:

Parent Signature: _____ **Date:** _____

Teacher name:
Teacher email:
Week of:

Parent Corner
Unit 4
Executive Functioning

We covered the following concepts in Unit 4:

- **Executive Functioning,** or EF, encompasses skills needed to be successful in life and can be challenging for middle school students—especially neurodivergent students. EF skills are vital to success in school, at work, and in relationships.
- The simple act of **making your bed** can have a ripple effect on other goals and successes throughout your day.
- It is important to **reflect** on your strengths and weaknesses in all areas, including the area of EF.
- Create **coping strategies** and use tools to compensate for areas of weakness. This can include using a planner or app (see suggestions below) to track your assignments, weekly grade checks and/or teacher check-ins, setting specific days of the week to get organized and check grades, using checklists, and more!

Next steps at home:

- Become aware of executive functioning topics (flexibility, leveled emotionality, impulse control, planning/organizing, and problem-solving) and continue to support your child in learning these life skills. Many of these are evident in everyday life, and you can help promote their mastering of these areas. The book *FLIPP the Switch* by Sheri Wilkins and Carol Burmeister (2015) is a good resource full of strategies to use at home.
- You guessed it: *require* your child to make their bed each day!
- Help your child reflect on their strengths and weaknesses in the area of EF. Remind them that no one is perfect!
- Help your child establish coping skills to compensate for their EF weaknesses.
- Model your own strengths and weaknesses and discuss how you compensate for them with coping strategies, just like they do.

Thank you for supporting PEERspective! By using the same vocabulary and reinforcing what is being taught, you will help your child generalize these skills much more effectively. Please don't hesitate to contact me at the above email if I can support you or your child in any way!

UNIT 5

"IT'S ALL ABOUT PERSPECTIVE!"
Using a Filter and Thinking Socially

I have to say, there is never a dull moment in my classroom. Just today, one of my students seemed proud to announce, "Mrs. Schmidt, my parents just ordered your book." I mean, how sweet is that? Then they said, "But I have no idea why." So close to a compliment ... so close. Rarely do I take these comments personally because, honestly, I know what they meant; why would their parents want to buy my first book, Why Didn't They Just Say That?, *when I had already told this student that the book is a teacher or therapist's guide to teaching social skills. Neither of the parents are teachers or therapists, so why the heck would they want that book?*

The comments made by students with autism are usually not meant maliciously but are due to a lack of perspective. This is a result of a theory of mind deficit (Baron-Cohen, Tager-Flusberg, & Lombardo, 2013). My student honestly didn't realize that you shouldn't tell the author of a book that you have no idea why someone would buy their life's work! Teaching perspective-taking and helping students learn to filter their thoughts and comments can be a daily challenge, but these students cannot fix something they don't realize they're doing.

Back to the complete obliteration of my ego mentioned in the above anecdote: After the student made the second comment, the entire class let out a collective "Ohhhh!" and someone pointed out that I had been "burned." I simply laughed and put the quote on my quote wall. Then, I took time to explain the why behind the class's reaction. While I cannot confidently say that that student will never inadvertently insult someone in the future, I can say that they will now be more aware of what they say. After all, they're going to have to look at their quote on the class quote wall the rest of the school year! Sweet revenge—just kidding!

Specific lessons include:

- Thanksgiving Perspective Lesson
- Book Talk
- Nonverbal Communication: Silent Movie
- Is It Okay to Lie?
- Being Socially Aware—Holiday Edition
- Stop, Think, and Filter

Unit 5: Using a Filter and Thinking Socially
Lesson 1: Thanksgiving Perspective Lesson

LESSON OBJECTIVES

1. Students will work to see other points of view and explain their point of view as well.
2. Students will work in groups and as a whole class to identify the different perspectives from each article.
3. Students will understand and be able to explain what perspective is.

RATIONALE

This lesson provides students with an opportunity to explore how different perspectives can affect a person's feelings and point of view on the same topic. Students will explore different perspectives on the history of Thanksgiving. Students then have an opportunity to annotate and answer perspective questions for their article. The questions help them understand that there are different points of view about this specific topic. Through class discussion, students will learn that the different perspectives address the questions differently, and that there are different points of view about the history of Thanksgiving. Students then take the perspective idea, apply it to current situations in their lives, and consider how those perspectives may be different through different situations with their family members, friends, teachers, etc.

LESSON OVERVIEW AND INSTRUCTION

Lesson Duration

One 45-minute class period

Lesson Materials

- Three different articles on the history of Thanksgiving
    - "The Wampanoag Side of the First Thanksgiving Story" (Tirado, 2018)
        - https://indiancountrytoday.com/archive/the-wampanoag-side-of-the-first-thanksgiving-story
    - "The First Thanksgiving" (National Geographic Kids, n.d.)
        - https://kids.nationalgeographic.com/history/article/first-thanksgiving

- o "The Pilgrims Were … Socialists?" (Zernike, 2010)
  - https://www.nytimes.com/2010/11/21/weekinreview/21zernike.html
- o Writing utensil
- Highlighter/annotation tool
- Perspective questions worksheet

Lesson Activity

1. Groups will receive an article about the history of Thanksgiving. The groups will read and annotate their article and answer questions about it.
2. Groups will then share their article and responses with classmates to discover how the different perspectives affect how they and their peers explore the origins of Thanksgiving.

Social Emotional Learning Competencies (CASEL, 2020) addressed in this lesson:

- Self-Awareness
- Self-Management
- Responsible Decision-Making
- Relationship Skills
- Social Awareness

Thanksgiving Perspective Lesson

Group Members: _____ Date: _____

What is *perspective*?

Read your article, and, as a group, respond to the questions below:

1. Briefly summarize the article:

2. How do the people described in this article feel about the Thanksgiving holiday?

3. Why do they feel this way?

4. How do you imagine you would feel about Thanksgiving if you were in their situation?

5. How can we apply the idea of taking someone else's perspective into our own lives?

Unit 5: Using a Filter and Thinking Socially
Lesson 2: Book Talk

LESSON OBJECTIVES

1. Students will read a text to learn about relevant content.
2. Students will complete the book discussion guide.
3. Students will make at least two comments during the book talk and respond in a thoughtful manner during discussion.
4. Students will work to see other points of view and explain their point of view as well.

RATIONALE

The students work intentionally on social skills throughout this lesson. Book talks enable students to have a shared experience and similar things to discuss. Students will share and discuss a set of questions provided to them prior to the book talk day, and each student is required to share their thoughts on the chapter. Although they will discuss the content that they read, the purpose of the book talk is not reading comprehension but the shared experience and exchange of ideas. Book discussion days offer a relaxed change of pace from the day-to-day curriculum.

LESSON OVERVIEW AND INSTRUCTION

Lesson Duration

One 45-minute period (this lesson is used multiple times throughout the year)

Lesson Materials

- Student Response page (provided beforehand and completed by each student prior to class)
- Pen, pencil, highlighter
- Sticky notes
    - Possible book for discussion: Michelle Garcia Winner and Pamela Crooke's *Social Fortune or Social Fate* (2011)

Lesson Activity

1. Students will sit at their desks, arranged in a circle, discussing a chapter from the selected text while enjoying a hot beverage and a snack.
2. Students are divided into pairs and are responsible for grading each other's participation. You can vary the requirements based on your class's needs, but students ought to make at least two thoughtful comments or takeaways from the chapter.
3. The partner setup allows peer coaches to prompt their partner and targeted students to see a model (by watching their partner) of how to meet the requirements.

Social Emotional Learning Competencies (CASEL, 2020) addressed in this lesson:

- Self-Awareness
- Self-Management
- Responsible Decision-Making
- Social Awareness

My Book Discussion Ideas

Name_____ Date_____

Pages/Chapter Title: _____

What I thought was useful:

What I didn't agree with or didn't understand:

Takeaways from the chapter:

How do I relate to this?

Quotes I can relate to: (use page numbers)

Unit 5: Using a Filter and Thinking Socially
Lesson 3: Nonverbal Communication—Silent Movie

LESSON OBJECTIVES

1. Students will be able to identify and interpret nonverbal communication.
2. Students will work in groups to write a topic or idea for a silent film.
3. Students will create short silent videos using their nonverbal body basics to convey their emotions.
4. Students will view their peers' videos and guess what they are doing based on the nonverbal communication.

RATIONALE

This lesson is used to help students better understand nonverbal communication skills in order to implement accurate perspective-taking. Nonverbals make up a large amount of communication in our lives. However, students on the spectrum often have difficulty interpreting nonverbal cues and understanding that their nonverbal cues and gestures can send messages to others. Reading and interpreting nonverbals takes perspective. Students must think about someone else's point of view based on their specific needs and wants, then determine what their nonverbals are "saying" to them, and adjust their actions accordingly. The students also need awareness of the messages that they are sending themselves with their bodies, eyes, and gestures in order to have effective communication.

LESSON OVERVIEW AND INSTRUCTION

Lesson Duration

Three 45-minute periods

Lesson Materials

- Journal
- Writing utensil
- Internet/device to show video clip

Lesson Activity

1. Students are shown various video clips that demonstrate visual representations of nonverbal communication and the resulting reactions of others.
   Example videos to use:
   - https://www.youtube.com/watch?v=9pOSvj4n6c4
   - https://www.youtube.com/watch?v=bWdyHMAtNMk
   - Scene from a silent Charlie Chaplin film
2. As students watch the videos, they write in their journals about what's happening and how they know this based on facial expressions, nonverbal communication, and on-screen interactions between people.
3. Using a provided rubric that details project expectations, groups of students then create their own silent movie script.
4. Students film their silent movie, focusing on the incorporation of nonverbals and other required elements as detailed in the rubric.

Social Emotional Learning Competencies (CASEL, 2020) addressed in this lesson:

- Self-Awareness
- Self-Management
- Relationship Skills
- Social Awareness

Silent Movie Project

Group Members: _____   Film Title: _____

	Excellent (10–8)	Great (7–6)	Good (5–3)	Poor (2–0)
Creativity	The students demonstrated their creativity by incorporating **at least five** nonverbal gestures and included **the use of props, video editing, and background music**.	The students demonstrated creativity by incorporating three or four nonverbal gestures and included the use of props and video editing or background music.	The students demonstrated their creativity by incorporating one to two nonverbal gestures and used props.	The students did not include any nonverbal gestures or props.
Collaboration	Collaboration is evident by having **each member of the group appear in the video at least once.** AND Each group member contributed to planning and editing the film.	Collaboration is evident by having 50% or more of the group members appear in the video. Some of the group members contributed to planning and editing the film.	Collaboration is evident by having 50% or fewer group members appear in the video, and only one group member contributed to editing the film.	Collaboration is lacking, with only one group member shown in the video.
Overall product	The film meets the **60-second time minimum, has a title**, and **has a clear beginning, middle, and end to the story**. The students remained on task when given class time for the project.	The film is 45–60 seconds in length, has a title, and has a beginning, middle, and end. The students remained on task for some of the time given in class.	The film is 45–60 seconds in length but does not show a clear beginning, middle, and end. The students were on task little of the time given in class.	The film is less than 45 seconds in length and does not have a clear beginning and end. The students were not on task when given class time to work on project.

Unit 5: Using a Filter and Thinking Socially
Lesson 4: Is It Okay to Lie?

LESSON OBJECTIVES

1. Students will read and utilize evidence from the text to better understand the concept of appropriate use of a lie in a specific social situation.
2. Students will interact and discuss the topic while utilizing the text to better to understand the social skill.
3. Students will provide specific social scenarios where using a small lie would be effective and appropriate.

RATIONALE

The concept of lying is difficult to understand for students with autism and other social skill struggles. This population often sees concepts as black or white, right or wrong. Looking for concrete evidence from the text to answer questions helps improve students' reading comprehension, and the concrete evidence helps students who see many things as black and white to understand that lying is sometimes necessary and effective. This concept requires a lot of meaningful discussion and is a lesson in which utilizing peers is essential for successful comprehension.

LESSON OVERVIEW AND INSTRUCTION

Lesson Duration

One 45-minute period

Lesson Materials

- Article: "Is It OK to Lie?" Scholastic's *Scope* magazine (Pierce, 2018) https://scope.scholastic.com/issues/2018-19/100118/Is-It-OK-to-Lie.html
- Pen/pencil/highlighter
- Article discussion questions

Lesson Activity

1. Students are given a copy of a magazine article that focuses on the essential question, "Is it okay to lie?" Students work in partners or groups to read the article and the accompanying visual cartoon.
2. Once they have read the article together, they are provided questions (see handout) to discuss and consider. After discussion, they write down their responses as a group.
3. Once each group has completed the questions, the class comes back together as a whole to go through the discussion questions. These questions are specifically designed to bring about the topic of whether it is okay to lie and in what specific types of situations.

Social Emotional Learning Competencies (CASEL, 2020) addressed in this lesson:

- Self-Awareness
- Self-Management
- Responsible Decision-Making
- Relationship Skills
- Social Awareness

Is it Okay to Lie? Article Discussion Questions

Name(s)_____ Date_____

Discuss the questions with your group and answer them below.

1. Which quote best supports the argument that lying is okay in certain situations?

    a. "Most Americans lie approximately twice a day."
    b. "'Most of the time, being kind to someone is more important than telling the absolute truth,' says Jane Frank, a psychologist in New York City."
    c. "Telling tiny lies, experts say, makes us more likely to tell bigger, more harmful lies in the future."
    d. "We depend on each other to be honest, and deceiving those we care about can damage our relationships."

2. Which claim could NOT be supported by information in the article?

    a. It's okay to lie if you are trying to protect someone's feelings.
    b. Americans lie often.
    c. Many people tell lies without knowing it.
    d. Telling one lie can lead to more lies.

3. What idea about lying does the accompanying cartoon express? Explain your answer:

4. How does this article relate to filtering your thoughts, ideas, and opinions when having conversations with family and friends?

Unit 5: Using a Filter and Thinking Socially
Lesson 5: Being Socially Aware, Holiday Edition

LESSON OBJECTIVES

1. Students will identify the most appropriate social move to utilize during specific social situations. They will also identify inappropriate actions during a social situation.
2. Students will demonstrate the social skill behaviors with visual supports to help identify the appropriate way to handle each holiday situation.

RATIONALE

Visual supports are used for students who struggle with social skill issues, as well as students with autism. Once students are able to identify the negative and then positive visuals, they should be able to demonstrate the social skill themselves in a real-world scenario.

LESSON OVERVIEW AND INSTRUCTION

Lesson Duration

>Two 45-minute periods

Lesson Materials

- Recording device (iPad, iPhone, Chromebook, etc.)
- Script paper
- Pencil/pen
- Holiday props

Lesson Activity

1. Begin the lesson by sharing and reviewing social skill video examples as a class relevant to the holiday season (see link below). In each example, the class will work together to identify what social skill is being used in the example scenarios.
    - https://www.youtube.com/playlist?list=PLGIcqu5UUAb3fc1bNhgqlt_-MrZKosoj0
2. After students have identified the social skills that the characters are using to be socially aware, they are assigned to work in various groups.

3. Each group will receive a different holiday scenario about which they will be asked to make two videos: One video will show the students not being socially aware during the holiday situation, while the second video will show them being more socially aware and using learned social skills to have a successful social interaction. While the social skill can be used at any time of the year, many such scenarios occur around the holidays, so this lesson utilized these types of examples:

   - Receiving a gift that you don't love
   - Eating an item from the holiday meal that you don't enjoy
   - When someone gives you a gift, but you didn't get them anything
   - When you want to open presents, but you have to follow the order of events from your family
   - Having a conversation with someone who celebrates the holidays differently than you do or does not celebrate a holiday

4. Students work together to create both video scripts and then film them.
5. The videos will then be shown and discussed as a class.

Social Emotional Learning Competencies (CASEL, 2020) addressed in this lesson:

- Self-Awareness
- Self-Management
- Responsible Decision-Making
- Relationship Skills
- Social Awareness

Unit 5: Using a Filter and Thinking Socially
Lesson 6: Stop, Think, and Filter

LESSON OBJECTIVES

1. Students will complete a journal and discuss it with their group.
2. Students will be able to recall the three questions they should ask before making a comment or asking a question.
3. Students will understand the connection between what they say and do and how others perceive those actions.
4. Students will filter their responses in multiple settings using the three questions.

RATIONALE

This lesson helps teach students that everyone has thoughts in their heads. Some thoughts are okay to share, but others should stay in our "thought bubble." The thought bubble journal page can be used as a single lesson or throughout the year. By having students journal the thoughts that they choose to filter throughout the day, you are teaching them that we all have thoughts and feelings we don't share and that we make choices about keeping thoughts in a thought bubble. After the students understand that everyone has these thoughts, then the three questions—Is it kind? Is it necessary? Can I wait to discuss this at a later time?—can be asked as a more concrete way to decide whether they should share. You can reinforce this lesson throughout the year by asking students, "Could that comment have been said at a different time?" and/or by posting visual reminders in your classroom or even at a student's desk.

LESSON OVERVIEW AND INSTRUCTION

Lesson Duration

One or two 45-minute periods

Lesson Materials

- Student journal for drafting ideas
- Pen, pencil
- Handouts

Lesson Activity

1. This lesson starts with a quiet, individual journal exercise, either in a physical journal or online. The prompt is, "Throughout the day, many thoughts and feelings pop into your head, and you get to choose which ones stay there! Remember, people have thoughts and feelings about you based on your words and actions. Record things you kept in your thought bubble below." Depending on when your class meets, you can adjust the journal to include any thoughts from the last 24 hours or the night before.
2. After the students have completed their journal entries, they can then share with their groups.
3. Conclude the first part of this lesson with a discussion about what types of things each group discussed (be sure to remind them to be school-appropriate).
4. Next, ask the students how they know whether to keep those particular thoughts in their "thought bubble."
5. Share the second handout, and teach the three questions they should ask themselves prior to verbalizing their thoughts: 1) Is it kind? 2) Is it necessary? 3) Can it wait for another time?

If you feel your students need more than one day on this topic, you can have them do skits and even record the skits. They can act out a thought they have and model the new filtering system (asking themselves one or more of the questions), show how they decided to keep it in their head, and then show the reactions of others around them. If you have a specific student who is working on this skill, you can have them keep the video to view later.

Social Emotional Learning Competencies (CASEL, 2020) addressed in this lesson:

- Self-Awareness
- Self-Management
- Relationship Skills
- Social Awareness

Filtering My Thoughts and Feelings   Name: _____

Journal: Throughout the day, many thoughts and feelings pop into your head, and you get to choose which ones stay there! Remember, people have thoughts and feelings about *you* based on your words and actions. Record things you kept in your thought bubble below.

STOP, Filter, and use your Thought Bubble!

Before I speak, I should ask myself these questions:

- ❑ Is it kind?
- ❑ Is it necessary?
- ❑ Can I wait to discuss this at a later time?

By filtering my thoughts and feelings, I get to choose how other people feel about me based on my words and actions!

This handout can be enlarged for a classroom visual or made into an individual visual prompt on a student's desk (with or without the artwork).

Unit 5: Using a Filter and Thinking Socially
Additional Activities and Ideas

- **Classroom Quote Wall:** One way to help establish rapport and learn that everyone looks at the world differently is to have a classroom quote wall. This wall contains quotes from students and teachers that are either funny or profound. This becomes a way to remember all the lessons learned throughout the school year, celebrate everyone's uniqueness, and provide inside jokes (which many of our students have never experienced). Be sure to set ground rules, such as only the teacher decides what goes on the quote wall and writes it on the board, if you are trying to get on the quote wall you will not get on the quote wall, etc. Being on the quote wall becomes a point of pride for students, which is a fun way to celebrate uniqueness and start some interesting conversations about language and meaning.

Our inside jokes and meaningful quotes are posted in our classroom all year on our Quote Wall.

- **Band App:** This is a free communication app for groups. The features include announcements, shared calendar, instant messaging, and class polls. By using a class app, the students don't have to exchange phone numbers or other information (unless they choose to), and they can communicate, stay involved, and even share photographs of outings and events. This is a great way for students to build rapport and learn to communicate on a form of social media with supervision and coaching.

- **T-shirts:** What better way to build on your classroom rapport than a good team t-shirt? Let students design a class t-shirt for the year. Students can vote on their favorite design, and the shirts can be used for class outings, field trips, or even just a random day at school to show class pride. Creating the t-shirt as a class allows students to create ownership of their class, build rapport, and support each other in their own ways.

The SCC club enjoys wearing their t-shirts as a group to school!

- **Morning Check-ins:** This provides an opportunity for students to get out any frustrations or negative feelings that they may want to share with you or with their peers. Making check-ins part of your everyday routine creates a safe zone for students and helps them to be more upfront when they are not feeling ready to learn. It also provides vital information for the teacher for that day, which helps prepare them (and the student's other teachers) for what their day may look like and why. This activity also provides good rapport for students and teachers. Middle school students love an opportunity to share, and by having this daily activity, they are more likely to participate in other class activities that day as well.

- **Slang/Pop Culture:** Slang is a type of informal language that is often difficult for our students to understand. This is particularly true with middle and high school students, who use ever-evolving slang terms in conversation among themselves and on social media. This type of communication is challenging to teach because slang terms change and evolve over time. You can consider teaching these definitions as they come up in lessons and conversations, or you can intentionally teach them by doing a "word of the day" and including slang along with figurative language. The purpose of teaching slang and figurative language is so that students understand conversations around them without necessarily encouraging them to use the terms on a regular basis.

- **School Community Involvement:** Encourage and even challenge students to become a bigger part of their school community. Take your class to any club fairs to encourage them to join and meet other students who have similar interests. If this is too big a leap, encourage them to be a part of their school community in smaller ways, such as participating in door-decorating contests, dressing up for spirit week, or voting for various things as they come up.

- **Coffee Filter:** Keep a coffee filter on hand and use it as a visual throughout the year to remind students to filter their thoughts. I would keep this tool for PEERspective class only and not use it in general classes the students may be in. PEERspective is a safe space where students can learn in real time when they lack a filter!

Teacher name:
Teacher email:
Week of:

Parent Corner
Unit 5
Using a Filter and Thinking Socially

We covered these concepts in Unit 5:

- We all have different **perspectives** based on our age, gender, and life experiences.
- Even **if we don't agree with someone's perspective**, we can use choice # 1—decide not to tell them we disagree with them (keep it in your thought bubble), or choice # 2—respectfully accept that they have a different opinion or perspective, and that is okay. Your thought bubble is a reference to an imaginary bubble above your head where you keep thoughts and feelings.
- Book Talks allow the students to practice annotating, backing ideas with text, **waiting** for a pause to speak, respectfully disagreeing, keeping comments in their thought bubble, and **filtering** thoughts to not monopolize the discussion.
- At times, a **white lie** can be the right thing to do socially, depending on the situation.

Next steps at home:

- Find opportunities to point out different perspectives. Show your child that you sometimes disagree with someone's point of view but choose to keep it in your thought bubble, for example.
- Prompt your child to use choice one or choice two above when navigating a different point of view or a social situation.
- Prompt your child to wait for a pause to speak and filter their thoughts and feelings in order to avoid monopolizing the conversation. This can be at home with immediate family, socializing with friends, or in a larger gathering of friends or family.
- Prior to a holiday or social event, remind your child to use their filters and be sure to make the right social decision, which sometimes will be a "white lie."

Thank you for supporting PEERspective! By using the same vocabulary and reinforcing what is being taught, you will help your child generalize these skills much more effectively. Please don't hesitate to contact me at the above email if I can support you or your child in any way!

UNIT 6

"INSTAGRAM IS REAL, RIGHT?"
Navigating Social Media in Middle School

Katie raised her hand in class and asked if she could take a selfie with her friends "as proof." While this was a little confusing to me, I realized it was of great importance to her, so I let her take the picture. Then she explained further that she was visiting her previous school soon, and she needed to show them all the friends she had now. While I loved the sentiment that she felt accepted in class and knew she had friends, I couldn't help but feel a little sad for this generation; it's almost like it isn't real unless it's documented or Instagrammed. Even as a mom, I often feel that I am missing out on enjoying one of my daughter's live performances because I am too concerned with capturing the moment on my phone to share later on Facebook (the "Instagram" for old people). So much pressure is put on our students these days, from posting the perfect selfie to getting your Tik Tok on the top of the page of your followers' attention; there is just a lot of demand in the illusive world of social media.

Students with autism are typically quite literal, which makes all of this even harder to navigate. If you are my "friend" on social media, are you also my "friend" at school? If that couple looks happy online, then they must be a happy couple, right? Over the years, many unfortunate situations have come up because of the confusion and false expectations involved in social media and phone usage in general. This chapter helps peer coaches teach the parameters and limits needed to safely navigate the ever-changing social world known as social media—yet another reason why having same-age peer coaches is vital!

Specific lessons include:

- Friendship Presentation
- Unwritten Rules of Social Media
- Social Media Thoughts and Feelings
- Cross the Line
- Social Media "How-To" Book

Unit 6: Navigating Social Media in Middle School
Lesson 1: Friendship Presentation

LESSON OBJECTIVES

1. Students will independently identify the different types of friendship and give an example for each section.
2. Students will identify important information relevant to online friendships.
3. Students will share important information as a group with their classmates to provide essential information about online friendships.

RATIONALE

This lesson addresses different levels of friendship and how friendship changes when it is paired with social media. Using a book written specifically from a student perspective, students learn about online friendships and can relate because they can imagine the experience from the point of view of a student who is just like them. Working in groups to identify and share the important information also creates a shared experience where the students become the experts, teaching their peers what they have learned.

LESSON OVERVIEW AND INSTRUCTION

Lesson Duration

Two 45-minute periods

Lesson Materials

- Chapter 5 of *Middle School: The Stuff Nobody Tells You About* (Moss, 2010)
- Student journal
- Pen/pencil
- Highlighter/sticky notes

Lesson Activity

1. The students are broken up into groups of 4 or 5 and assigned specific sections from Chapter 5 of *Middle School: The Stuff Nobody Tells You About* (Moss, 2010). This chapter is 37 pages long and can be broken up into what fits best for your student groupings and needs.
2. Student groups read and annotate their section of the chapter for important parts that they will put into a presentation to share with their peers.
3. While they are sharing, peers will take notes on the important parts that they hear. The class will eventually work together to create their own how-to social media book on friendships; taking good notes now will help them create their how-to books at a later date.

Social Emotional Learning Competencies (CASEL, 2020) addressed in this lesson:

- Self-Awareness
- Self-Management
- Responsible Decision-Making
- Relationship Skills
- Social Awareness

Students work together to determine the unwritten rules of social media!

Unit 6: Navigating Social Media in Middle School
Lesson 2: Unwritten Rules of Social Media

LESSON OBJECTIVES

1. Students will take guided notes on different types (or levels) of friendships.
2. Students will work in groups to identify the unwritten rules for their assigned type of friendship.
3. Students will present their specific level and unwritten rules for that level to their peers.
4. Students will take notes on the different rules for the levels as presented to them.

RATIONALE

Students will learn about the unwritten rules of social media to inform their social awareness as they navigate online worlds. They will utilize the guided notes and the unwritten rules to help them make the rules more personal to their daily interactions with different types of friends and different friendships on social media. Working in groups to identify these rules will help students understand that these rules are what they need to follow and use throughout their middle school interactions with different peers. The different examples also provide students with strong visuals that they can take with them in making their own rules and in their daily middle school lives interacting with various peers on various levels.

LESSON OVERVIEW AND INSTRUCTION

Lesson Duration

Two 45-minute periods

Lesson Materials

- Student journal
- Friendship PowerPoint Guided Notes found on Google Drive
- Pen/pencil
- Highlighter/sticky notes

Lesson Activity

1. Students will initially take guided notes on the different types of friendships they encounter in middle school. This can be completed in a variety of ways; you can provide guided notes, or you can have students copy directly into their journals. Throughout the guided notes, real middle school examples are given of different friendships that students encounter daily. These will be provided to help them connect with the notes.
2. Once students have taken notes, they will create unwritten rules that they encounter with the different levels of friendships. Students are divided into six groups for the six different levels where they can utilize the examples given and their guided notes, and then discuss which unwritten rules apply to each type of friendship and what that type looks like.
3. Once they decide on their unwritten rules, students will type them up in a shared document. They can make this document their own by working together as a group to create their own fonts, visuals, etc.
4. Once they have created their document, which can serve as a visual of the different levels of friendship for their own reference, they can share this with the rest of the class. The students don't know this yet, but they have also created rules that they will share in their final project for this unit, where they create their own social media how-to book about friends and online friendships in lesson 5 of this unit.

Social Emotional Learning Competencies (CASEL, 2020) addressed in this lesson:

- Self-Awareness
- Relationship Skills
- Social Awareness

Unit 6: Navigating Social Media in Middle School
Lesson 3: Social Media Thoughts and Feelings

LESSON OBJECTIVES

1. Students will work effectively in groups to collaborate and share ideas.
2. Students will read each note card to determine how that comment/post made them feel.
3. Students will articulate to the class what the note card says while stating how it made them feel.

RATIONALE

This lesson is designed to assist students in realizing what they should and should not post or comment on their social media pages. Social media can be an outlet for many middle school and high school students. However, some students are still learning to understand that everything that is posted has an effect on others. During the discussion, students may also discover if the note card leaves a classmate with a different feeling. This activity gives students the opportunity to understand that everything they say online has an effect.

LESSON OVERVIEW AND INSTRUCTION

Lesson Duration

One 45-minute class period

Lesson Materials

- Prepared printouts or note cards with social media comments (provided on the following handout)

Lesson Activity

1. The students are divided into small groups and sit together at one table. Students will be handed ten note cards with different comments and posts copy/pasted from social media or written down by the teacher.
2. Groups will have 20 minutes to read each note card and determine what type of feeling the comment leaves them with. Students have a list of different emotions written on the board that they will choose from to describe each comment/post written on each note card.

3. After groups have determined the feeling categories for all the note cards, the class will come together. Each student will read a note card aloud to the class, share what emotion the group gave it, and explain the reasoning for the feeling they chose to represent that comment.
4. The lesson should conclude with a discussion of how every comment provoked a thought or feeling for each student.

Social Emotional Learning Competencies (CASEL, 2020) addressed in this lesson:

- Self-Awareness
- Self-Management
- Relationship Skills
- Social Awareness

UNIT 6: "INSTAGRAM IS REAL, RIGHT?"   147

Examples of Comments Made on Social Media

Be sure to make your own comments appropriate to the students' ages.

These can be photocopied and cut out or written on note cards, but either way, more than the provided comments will likely be needed.

"You look so confident."	"Ummm … I don't know what to think about this photo. I just don't like it at all."
"Did you photoshop this?"	"Why are you hanging out with her again?"
"This picture is not flattering at all."	"Congrats on getting MVP!"
"You go, girl!"	"Why would you wear those shorts!"

Unit 6: Navigating Social Media in Middle School
Lesson 4: Cross the Line

LESSON OBJECTIVES

1. Students will understand the concept of a digital footprint and why it is important to have a good social media presence by watching and discussing a video.
2. Students will identify examples of posts that would be socially appropriate (not crossing the line) and posts that would not be socially appropriate (crossing the line) by using a visual to guide and collaborating with peers.

RATIONALE

The lesson's purpose is to teach students to distinguish between socially appropriate and socially inappropriate social media posts. This is important because social media lets people post things that could negatively affect people's perception of them and could also hurt others. Teaching this concept through visuals and examples allows for all individuals to think, reflect, and connect to their posts to ensure they are maintaining a positive social media presence.

LESSON OVERVIEW AND INSTRUCTION

Lesson Duration

One 45-minute class period

Lesson Materials

- YouTube video: https://www.youtube.com/watch?v=ottnH427Fr8
- A wall, poster board, chalkboard, dry-erase board, or other space to tape responses
- Photos to use as examples of social media posts
- Tape

Lesson Activity

1. The teacher will begin the lesson by sharing a video about the concept of digital footprints https://www.youtube.com/watch?v=ottnH427Fr8.

2. Following the video, the teacher will ask a discussion question of the entire group: "What do you think the term *oversharing* means when thinking about posts on social media?" The students will discuss this question with their peers in groups of 3 to 4.
3. After group discussion, bring the discussion back to the whole class. The teacher will then transition to a discussion of "crossing the line" in relation to the term "oversharing." The teacher will draw a line or use a line of tape on the board to have a visual of "crossing the line" for all students.
4. The teacher will pass out screenshots or photos of posts from various social media platforms to each table. Each group should be given at least five posts to analyze. Some examples of these posts may include things such as political commentary, memes, status updates, Snapchats, comments on photos, etc.
    Recommendation: Choose a variety of pictures that give a broad range of things that are socially acceptable to post on social media versus posts that would be considered unacceptable.
5. After having some time to think and collaborate as a group, the students will be asked to bring their posts to the wall, share the post with the group, and then tape the photo to the wall where it belongs based on whether it has "crossed the line" or if it is considered appropriate to post on social media). The class as a whole may discuss and agree or disagree with the place it was posted on the board. This should prompt a good discussion in which people get to explain their thoughts and learn from their peers.
6. After this activity, discuss as a class why having a good presence on social media is important. Connect this back to the video and the discussion on digital footprints. If there is time, have students record in a journal or on paper what they want their digital footprint to look like.

Social Emotional Learning Competencies (CASEL, 2020) addressed in this lesson:

- Self-Awareness
- Self-Management
- Responsible Decision-Making
- Social Awareness

Unit 6: Navigating Social Media in Middle School
Lesson 5: Social Media How-To Book

LESSON OBJECTIVES

1. Students will identify the most important information they have learned over the course of this unit and create documents to share.
2. Students will collaborate to determine important information to include in their assigned section.

RATIONALE

This is a great wrap-up lesson to complete toward the end of the social media unit! Students combine their newfound knowledge to create a culminating project in the form of a class-created book. By creating such a project, students take ownership of their learning to identify the most important information in the unit. By creating and explaining the information, students are able to feel like the teachers and take ownership of their learning. This reinforces the main points learned from this social media unit.

LESSON OVERVIEW AND INSTRUCTION

Lesson Duration

Two to three 45-minute periods

Lesson Materials

- Computer paper
- Pencil
- Utensils in different colors
- Word processing platform

Lesson Activity

1. Students are divided into groups to identify essential information to include in a section of a social media how-to book that will be created by the whole class.
    The sections assigned to each group could include:

    - Types of online friendships
    - Tips and tricks for friend requests
    - Tips and tricks for communicating online (Facebook, Instagram, Twitter, etc.)
    - Tips and tricks for sharing personal information on the internet
    - Tips and tricks to avoid online scams
    - Tips and tricks for texting in a group conversation with people you may not know
    - Tips and tricks for texting a guy or girl that you may like as more than a friend
    - Tips and tricks for texting a friend who is sick at home
    - Tips and tricks for interacting on social media/texting with close friends
    - Tips and tricks for being ghosted (ignored)

2. Groups will work together to decide the most important information to include in their section and use their creativity to provide graphics and drawings to accompany their section.
3. After a plan has been made, provide students with time to complete the tasks associated with their section.
4. Finally, the class can work together to make a cover page for the booklet.
5. After completion, combine the pages from each group and give a copy to every student.

Social Emotional Learning Competencies (CASEL, 2020) addressed in this lesson:

- Self-Awareness
- Responsible Decision-making
- Relationship Skills
- Social Awareness

Social Media How-To Book

Name_____ Date_____

Our class has become the new leading experts when it comes to handling social media in the most appropriate way possible. Now it's time to share your knowledge with the world! Working in groups, we will make our own "how-to" book for middle school students everywhere.

Our class will include the following topics in our book (circle the topics assigned to your group):

- Types of online friendships
- Tips and tricks for friend requests
- Tips and tricks for communicating online (Facebook, Instagram, Twitter, etc.)
- Tips and tricks for sharing personal information on the internet
- Tips and tricks to avoid online scams
- Tips and tricks for texting in a group conversation with some people you may not know
- Tips and tricks for texting a guy or girl that you may like as more than a friend
- Tips and tricks for texting a friend who is sick at home
- Tips and tricks for interacting on social media/texting with close friends
- Tips and tricks for being ghosted (ignored)

Don't forget as a class you also need to include:

- Visuals for your topic
- Cover page
- Visuals with color throughout the how-to book

Participation from every student is critical!

My group's section is due: _____

Our final class draft is due: _____

Unit 6: Navigating Social Media in Middle School Additional Activities and Ideas

- **Email etiquette:** Students sometimes struggle to maintain a professional tone in emails to teachers, coaches, and peers. Be sure to cover topics such as avoiding emailing as though you are texting (e.g., using terms like LOL) and having an age-appropriate email address (no more Lovesanimals@outlook.com). Practicing appropriate email is a vital skill for the future and should be covered throughout the year (starting with the "About Me" email mentioned in unit 1 and revisited throughout the school year).

- **Emoji 101:** Consider doing a lesson about the meanings behind emojis used in texting and social media. For example, if I am friends with a peer and I put the "heart eye emoji" as a comment on one of their social media posts, I could be indicating that I like them in a romantic way; this can really confuse our students with autism who don't understand the unwritten meanings of things like emojis, and they sometimes become easy targets online when they misunderstand what they are "saying" when posting comments that include emojis.

- **Parental controls:** Remind parents that they should have their child's passwords on all accounts and check the content regularly. This gets trickier as the students get older, so setting this standard early is helpful when they are first learning to navigate various types of social media. Many tools and applications are available for parents to help teach their middle school child to navigate social media in a safe and productive way; here are a couple examples:

    1. **Pocket Points app:** This application keeps track of time spent on social media. Parents can use this app to challenge their children to limit their use and to offer incentives to stay off their phone. This app is similar to the Screen Time setting on Apple products.
    2. **Rethink app:** This application was created by a high school student. It searches for certain keywords, then asks the user, "Are you sure you want to send this?" More than 40 percent of the messages do not get sent after users receive this prompt, so this app can act as an external filter.

- **Social media share time:** Choose one day a week (Fridays work well) when students can share something from social media. This is a great way to expose all the students to various types of social media and the purpose behind it. Of course, you must be careful to ensure what is being shared is school-appropriate, so be sure to review it yourself ahead of time. This preview stage can lead to good one-on-one discussions with individual students about what's appropriate and what isn't. Discussions like this are helpful for teaching perspective-taking.

- **Social media encompasses the following outlets but is always evolving. Any/all of these platforms, or newly emerged ones, are relevant for discussion:**

    1. Facebook (Please note: Most middle schoolers, if they're on Facebook at all, tend to use it for staying in touch with family, not interacting with their friends.
    2. Instagram
    3. Twitter
    4. Tik Tok
    5. Snapchat
    6. YouTube
    7. Online games such as Minecraft and Fortnight; these are games, but players interact and play together, so there are social aspects involved.

Teacher name:
Teacher email:
Week of:

Parent Corner
Unit 6

Navigating Social Media in Middle School

We covered the following concepts in Unit 6:

- There are different types of friendships: friendly bystanders, acquaintances, part-time friends, close friends, and best friends. Both people must want to move to the next level in order for the friendship to evolve.
    o Just because someone is nice to you once, it doesn't mean that they are now your best friend. This is **type #1, *Friendly***.
- There are many **unwritten rules** with regard to friendships!
- Online friendship and in-person friendship are not created equal.
    o **Be very careful** when posting online because people have thoughts and feelings about you based on what you say, do, and post.
    o Be careful not to overshare online. Look back at your Social Media How-To book for guidelines and parameters.

Next steps at home:

- When your child is talking about a friend, help them determine what "level" the friendship currently is and what to do to move to the next level (if they want to). In other words, if your child has an "acquaintance" and wants to have a "possible friend," encourage them to plan a social outing to spend time with the peer.
- Monitor your child's social media presence and have open discussions about what to post and what should remain in your head to be discussed only with your family.
- Discuss online safety and social etiquette with your child often, using specific examples when possible.
- Remind your child to look back at the Social Media How-To book for guidelines and parameters.

Thank you for supporting PEERspective! By using the same vocabulary and reinforcing what is being taught, you will help your child generalize these skills much more effectively. Please don't hesitate to contact me at the above email if I can support you or your child in any way!

UNIT 7

"WHY CAN'T I DO THAT ANYMORE?"

Growing Up, Changing Rules, and Transition

"Excuse me, Ms. Barrett. I am not sure how to tell you this, but Mark has his pants on, um, backwards."
—Just another day in the life of a teacher of our amazing students! Megan quietly whispered to Mark that his pants were on backward, which he protested against loudly until he looked down and discovered that his pants were indeed on backward.

Often students on the spectrum, like Mark, don't take the time to notice (or care) how they look or are perceived by their peers, due largely in part to a theory of mind deficit (Baron-Cohen, Tager-Flusberg, & Lombardo, 2013). But age-appropriate social skills go beyond personal hygiene. When I first started at Beavercreek High School, I noticed that often our students find comfort in items associated with their special interest. For example, one particular student, Grant, was into the military and is now quite successful after enlisting in his chosen field; however, on many occasions during his high school classes, I had to tell him to please put his army men away. Despite my reminders, when I'd look away, he'd be back at it again. This is a young man who took general and advanced classes, had friends, and was in JROTC; it was not age-appropriate for him to be playing with army men in high school.

While part of me considers it a good thing that these students sometimes lack any concern about being judged socially, the unfortunate fact is that if we want to help them fit in—now and in the future—they must accept that how we look, and what we say and do, impacts those around us and causes them to have thoughts about us. These thoughts are either good, bad, or neutral, and we should aim for good or at least neutral thoughts. It is important to teach that what is appropriate in elementary school or at home isn't necessarily appropriate at middle school. Social rules are already confusing enough, but now we need to teach that the rules change based on age and environment.

Over the years, many students have asked me some version of the same question: "How do all the other students just innately know what to do socially?" The answer, of course, is that they don't. They learn it too. But if you think about it, there is some validity to this comment. Often our perspective is that others have it all figured out. When other people appear to have it all together, we assume that is the reality of the situation; for students with autism who struggle with social awareness and theory of mind deficit, it can be difficult to understand that what you see isn't exactly what you get (Baron-Cohen, Tager-Flusberg, & Lombardo, 2013). We need to ensure that our students realize that other people might be faking it, and they can, too!

The idea of "faking it till you make it" helps everyone. My friend Sarah Beck first told me to "fake it till you make it" when she was training me and helping me prepare for my first half-marathon. I remember talking with her and another friend about wrapping my brain around running 13.1 miles, when the most I'd run up to that point was 10 miles. She told me that the last 3.1 (and don't forget the .1) was just faking it till you make it miles. I literally chanted (don't worry, it was in my head) "fake it till you make it" the last 3.1 miles of that race!

With social skills, it's a similar thing; we have to lift our chin up, throw our shoulders back, and fake it till we make it. I remind my students often that if they don't know what to do in a given social situation, they should look around and observe the expected social behavior, and do that. This social stuff can be confusing, but there are some tricks that can help you look like you know exactly what to do. This unit is all about those tricks.

Specific lessons include:

- Filter It or Say It?
- Awareness Matters
- Awareness Matters, Part 2
- Rules Change with Age: Picture Book Project
- Emotion Matching Game
- Scavenger Hunt

Unit 7: Growing Up, Changing Rules, and Transition
Lesson 1: Filter It or Say It?

LESSON OBJECTIVES

1. Students will discuss and determine if statements are thoughts that are socially appropriate to say out loud or thoughts that should remain in their head.
2. Students will discuss in groups, and as a whole class, their reasons for classifying each thought into the two categories.
3. Students will be able to personally reflect on these thoughts and share any personal connections to this concept.

RATIONALE

Students at the middle school level are learning social norms and expectations of them as they transition from the elementary level and eventually head to high school. Many of them struggle with the social aspects of middle school—especially when it comes to identifying appropriate comments to say in groups with their peers, teachers, and friends at school. In this lesson, they can discuss the reasoning for both sides, as well as share conversations with their peers about the idea of filtering and why it is vital to social success at middle school and beyond.

LESSON OVERVIEW AND INSTRUCTION

Lesson Duration

One 45-minute period

Lesson Materials

- Filter It/Say It! chart
- Statement/comment strips handout
- Scissors
- Glue

Lesson Activity

1. The students will be divided into groups. The groups will receive a piece of paper that lists 16 different thoughts.
2. The students will read each thought and determine whether it is a statement they could say out loud to a peer—meaning it would be socially acceptable to say it—or a statement that should remain a thought in their own head. Students can discuss and come to an agreement on each statement (or thought).
3. After they have agreed, they will cut out and glue each statement to the appropriate side of the chart.
4. After each group has completed their chart, the class as a whole discusses each statement to ensure that students can check their thinking and understanding and adjust their strips as needed for future reference if they find themselves in that specific situation.

Social Emotional Learning Competencies (CASEL, 2020) addressed in this lesson:

- Self-Awareness
- Self-Management
- Responsible Decision-Making
- Relationship Skills
- Social Awareness

Filter It, Say It!

Name_____ Date_____

FILTER IT	SAY IT

Filter It, Say It!

You are such a nerd. I can't believe you watch that show.
I'm frustrated and I need a break!
I need some help on this math assignment—I'm having a hard time with it.
Do you want to hang out this weekend and watch a movie?
Ew, you smell. Get away from me!
I really like your drawings. They are beautiful.
You can't sit at this lunch table—you aren't cool enough!
Wow, you are the biggest idiot I know. I can't believe you didn't know that answer.
Hey, I know that you think what the teacher said is funny, but could you laugh a little quieter? The loudness is really disruptive to me.
You're doing the project wrong! That's not how I wanted to do it!
Your haircut is definitely different! If it makes you feel good, then I love it!
I hate that shirt that you have on. It is super ugly and a terrible color on you.
You made me so mad! We are not friends anymore!
I'm disappointed that you didn't talk to me first before changing our plans on Friday.
I really appreciate how nice you were to me in Social Studies today. Thanks for asking me to be in your group.
Your laugh is the most annoying laugh ever. Super annoying. No one likes it!

Unit 7: Growing Up, Changing Rules, and Transition
Lesson 2: Awareness Matters

LESSON OBJECTIVES

1. Students will watch videos and hypothesize what each character may be thinking and why.
2. Students will discuss their opinions with their peers.
3. Students will respect other group's guesses and listen to their rationale.

RATIONALE

One deficit area for most people with autism is difficulty understanding theory of mind (TOM) (Baron-Cohen, Tager-Flusberg, & Lombardo, 2013). TOM is linked to the ability to understand someone else's perspective or point of view, which plays a large role in social awareness. This lack of social awareness can cause the students to seem egocentric, which is rarely the case. Teaching students with autism to stop and think about other people's perspectives isn't easy, but it is vital to their future success. Using video modeling and mapping can be helpful when teaching this skill. This lesson should be repeated several times throughout the year with clips or actual incidents that happen in the school community.

LESSON OVERVIEW AND INSTRUCTION

Lesson Duration

Two to three 45-minute class periods

Lesson Materials

- Video clips (links below) and platform to show them
- *Awareness Matters Social Map* handout for each student

Lesson Activity

1. The students will be divided into pairs: a targeted student and a peer coach. These pairs will work together after watching each clip.
2. The students will identify what the designated characters may have been thinking. After some discussion, they can put their guess on the handout.

3. After each group has finished, discuss the groups' answers as a whole class. Be sure to ask each pair WHY they inferred that the person might be thinking what they have listed.
4. Then move on to the next clip, with students filling out a new handout.

This activity can take several class periods because of the discussion. Be sure to share with your class that each pair's guess is just that, a guess, so there is no debating and no right answer. As you might imagine, that is not an easy concept for your students with autism! But you don't want to waste any time arguing. You can use the links provided below, or you can find links to teach specific social situations.

Social Emotional Learning Competencies (CASEL, 2020) addressed in this lesson:

- Self-Awareness
- Self-Management
- Relationship Skills
- Social Awareness

Links to Videos:

One-upper: https://www.youtube.com/watch?v=NCjjx8A-jfE
Stop at 2:38
Characters: Penelope, Jim, Randy, and the instructor
This clip is an exaggeration of someone who makes too many comments and tries too hard to convince others that they are accomplished. This clip can be used by pausing the clip and showing the other characters' reactions to Penelope.

Making inappropriate jokes: https://www.youtube.com/watch?v=T3YkqbP-4ao
You can play this whole clip.
Characters: Michael, Pam, and Ryan
Joking with others can be challenging because so many variables go into joking. How well you know someone (level or type of friendship), age, setting, and other factors all impact teasing someone. This clip illustrates that Michael should not have joked with Pam at work, in front of a coworker, about something so serious. There are many clips from *The Office* that illustrate what *not* to do socially, so this series is a go-to when teaching social skills using short video clips. You can search YouTube as problems arise with your students throughout the year and literally show them what not to do! (Thanks, Michael Scott!)

Awareness Matters Social Map

Name_____ Date_____

Write a brief description of the scenario in the rectangle and then each person's name in the circles. Next to each person's name, write a possible perspective. If you don't have enough room, feel free to draw this mini-map on another sheet of paper.

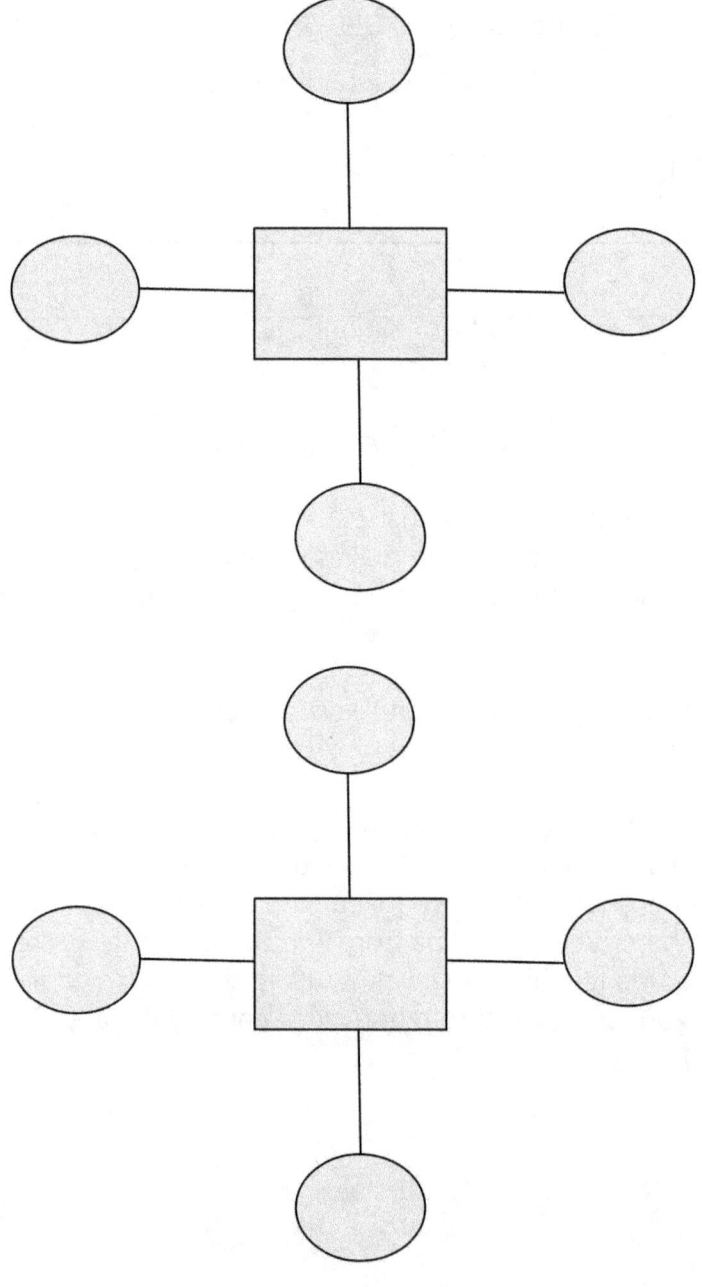

UNIT 7: "WHY CAN'T I DO THAT ANYMORE?" 165

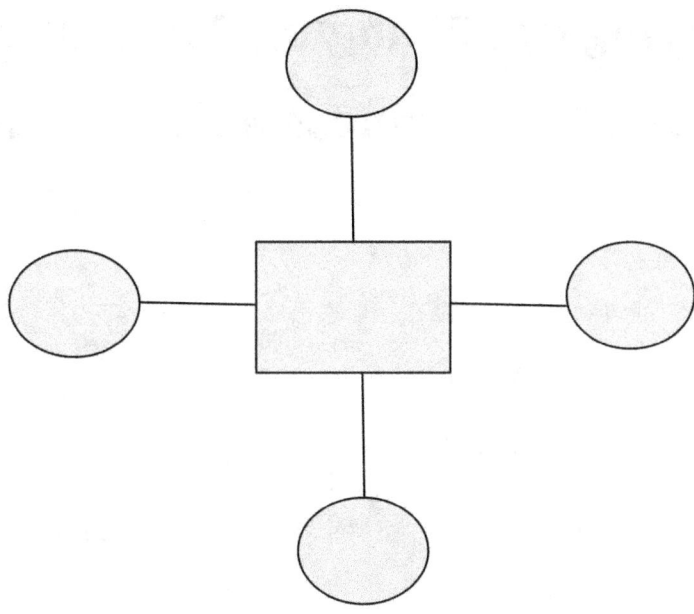

Remember, you are just making an informed guess or hypothesis about what people are thinking; it may or may not be accurate. Just do your best.

Unit 7: Growing Up, Changing Rules, and Transition
Lesson 3: Awareness Matters, Part 2

LESSON OBJECTIVES

1. Students will listen to each scenario and hypothesize what each person may be thinking and why.
2. Students will discuss their hypothesis with a partner.
3. Students will decide what hypothesis they would like to list on their perspective map.
4. Students will respect other groups' guesses and listen to their rationale.

RATIONALE

As discussed throughout the unit, social awareness is often a deficit for people with autism. Lack of perspective-taking can cause students to seem egocentric, which is rarely the case. Teaching students with autism to stop and think about other people's perspectives isn't easy, but it is vital to their future success. This follow-up lesson allows students to continue their work on perspective-taking using evidence-based practices. They can use this technique throughout their life, and the teacher can use this same visual to help dissect any social situations that come up during the school year as well.

LESSON OVERVIEW AND INSTRUCTION

Lesson Duration

One to two 45-minute class periods

Lesson Materials

- Awareness Matters, Part 2 Handout: "What Were They Thinking?!"
- Awareness Matters Social Map copies (from Part 1)

Lesson Activity

1. As with the previous lesson, the students will be divided into pairs (always pair a targeted student with a peer coach). These pairs will work together after hearing the scenarios presented on

the handout. The students will identify what the designated people may have been thinking. After some discussion, they can put their guess on the worksheet.
2. After each group has finished, discuss the answers of each group as a whole class. Be sure to ask each pair WHY they have inferred that the person may be thinking what they have listed.
3. After completing two or three provided scenarios, ask the students to write down their own scenario to share with the class (can be real or fictional). Remind the students to change the names of the people involved if they are using an actual situation.
4. You can have each pair share their scenario and allow the other students to map it out, or you can collect these scenarios and use them as quick follow-up reinforcement lessons throughout the unit. Either way, the students are learning social awareness through other people's perspectives, and they may even get to hear their peers' opinions on something they have actually experienced if they provided a real-life example.

Social Emotional Learning Competencies (CASEL, 2020) addressed in this lesson:

- Self-Awareness
- Self-Management
- Responsible Decision-Making
- Relationship Skills
- Social Awareness

Awareness Matters: What Were They Thinking?!

Name_____ Date_____

Working with a partner, and using the Awareness Matters Social Map handout provided, decide what perspective each of the following people had in the given scenario.

Scenario #1: Jalen is walking around the corner past the "No Students At Lunch" sign to go to Mrs. Schmidt's room to eat his lunch as he did the previous year. The security guard stops him and tells him to go back to the lunch room. Jalen refuses and gets very frustrated with the security guard. He ends up in the principal's office for insubordination.

Scenario #2: Hilary is walking down the hallway between classes and notices her principal's name tag has his first name on it. She loudly says, "What's up, Dan?" which makes her peers laugh. Her principal, who now seems annoyed, says, "Hilary, you cannot refer to adults by their first name." She responds, "Then why is it on your name tag?"

Scenario #3: Elyse is walking down the hallway heading to her next class when a big football player comes around the corner and knocks her down. Elyse screams that she's being bullied by the football team again when he leans down toward her. The teacher on hall duty runs over to help Elyse pick up her books and get to class.

Scenario #4: Jermeko is a part of a four-student group in science class assigned to build a structure that would prevent an egg from breaking when dropped from a four-foot counter. During the first work session, the team brainstorms ideas and narrows their strategy down to three options. Jermeko is gifted in science, so he goes home and makes all three protocols and brings them to class the next day. Jermeko doesn't understand why his group members are mad and why the teacher says she won't accept his work.

Scenario #5: Now it's your turn! In the space provided below, write your own scenario. It could be an actual situation that one of you experienced, or you can make something up. Be sure that there can be **at least two perspectives,** and **change the names** if it is something that really happened. Remember, it's all about perspective!

Unit 7: Growing Up, Changing Rules, and Transition
Lesson 4: Rules Change with Age Picture Book Project

LESSON OBJECTIVES

1. Students will identify appropriate times to express emotions.
2. Students will determine the physical characteristics of an assigned emotion.
3. Students will work in groups to create a visual to show an assigned emotion.
4. Students will share their storybooks with their peers and participate in a class discussion.

RATIONALE

This lesson takes students back to their picture book days. Never underestimate the powerful impact of a picture book! This specific picture book does a good job of illustrating one's emotions when feeling upset or "grumpy." It provides visuals for students who may not initially notice or understand what facial expressions are being shown. Specifically, they may not be aware that these facial expressions are more prominent and noticeable and picked up on by others the older they get; while it might be cute as a young child to show off your angry expressions to others, it is less socially acceptable as a middle school student. This lesson implements the strong use of visuals for our students to work on identifying emotions and the appropriate time to demonstrate these emotions, along with how appropriate expression of emotions changes as we age.

LESSON OVERVIEW AND INSTRUCTION

Lesson Duration

Two 45-minute periods

Lesson Materials

- Picture book: *Grumpy Monkey* by Suzanne Lang (2018)
- Student journal
- Coloring utensils
- Typing platform

Lesson Activity

1. This lesson begins with the teacher reading aloud the picture book *Grumpy Monkey* (Lang, 2018); a read-aloud version can be found on YouTube if desired. As the teacher reads the book, students write in their journals the different pictures that were shown in the book to illustrate the grumpy emotion. They can even draw their own pictures to show what they saw in the book and what it reminded them of.
2. Students will share what they wrote or drew in their journals.
3. Next, the students will be introduced to their own picture book project, where they will work in groups to display visuals of different emotions that they, as middle schoolers, may have. They will create their own story line and pictures. The following emotions are suggested for this project:

   - Sad/depressed
   - Angry
   - Happy/content
   - Excited
   - Worried/anxious

4. After assigning an emotion to each group, the groups may begin brainstorming for their picture book. They should come up with the physical signs of the assigned emotion and use those to create their story line and illustrations.
5. After completion, they can share their picture books with their classmates. You could even make it like a book club meeting, where snacks and beverages are provided while they share.

Social Emotional Learning Competencies (CASEL, 2020) addressed in this lesson:

- Self-Awareness
- Self-Management
- Relationship Skills
- Social Awareness

Rules Change with Age: Picture Book Project

Name_____ Date_____

Time to head back to your childhood roots and create a picture book of your own to share with your classmates! You just saw how the Grumpy Monkey displays one of his emotions. It's time for you to show what those emotions might look like in a storybook of your own. You will work together in groups to create your own story and pictures that demonstrate an assigned emotion. The possible emotions are (circle your assigned emotion)

- Sad/depressed
- Angry
- Happy/content
- Excited
- Worried/anxious

Picture Book Checklist

1. Determine the physical signs of your assigned emotion.
2. Create a story line with a clear beginning, middle, and end to show that emotion. Tell your story from a middle school perspective.
3. Remember that picture books are simple stories. Don't make it too complicated!
4. Create colored visuals that show this emotion and go along with your story line.
5. Present final project in class during a book club talk!

My final picture book is due: _____

Book club story time is: _____

Unit 7: Growing Up, Changing Rules, and Transition
Lesson 5: Emotion Matching Game

LESSON OBJECTIVES

1. Students will practice using different tones of voice and body language.
2. Students will practice reading the tone of others.
3. Students will practice identifying and using body language as it aligns with emotions.

RATIONALE

Students with autism often struggle to understand tone of voice and the meaning behind various tones and body language. In this activity, they can work on tone of voice and facial expressions in a fun way. By using phrases that don't have meaning or emotion connected to them, the students can practice showing meaning through the tone of their voices and expressions.

LESSON OVERVIEW AND INSTRUCTION

Lesson Duration

15–30 minutes

Lesson Materials

- 2 baskets, bins, or other containers for sorting
- 15–20 emotions listed on paper
- 20+ statements/questions listed on paper

Lesson Activity

1. Prepare 20 or more statements/questions about anything on cut-up strips of paper. Put them in one bin marked "Sentences." In another bin marked "Emotions," place slips of papers that individually list 15–20 different emotions.
2. The first player takes a card from the sentences bin and one card out of the emotions bin; they now must say that statement or question using the emotion listed on their card. They can use body language to help get the message across to the listeners.

3. The listeners each take a turn guessing the emotion listed on the card; whoever guesses correctly gets a point, and so does the speaker.
4. The person who guessed correctly then describes how they knew the emotion. If no one guesses correctly, then the speaker does not get a point.
5. Whoever has the most points at the end wins the game. The cards can be placed back in the bins to be used again (hopefully with another emotion).

Rules: You cannot choose another emotion because it is too difficult of a combination. You can choose another emotion/sentence card only if that same combination was already used during the game.

Social Emotional Learning Competencies (CASEL, 2020) addressed in this lesson:

- Self-Awareness
- Self-Management
- Social Awareness

Emotion Matching Game

Directions: Teachers or participants should prepare 20 or more statements they can use to practice tone and body language skills. For example: "We're going back to school tomorrow." These sentences will be paired with the emotions listed below, and players will then guess what emotion the player is expressing based on their tone of voice and body language.

Happy	Nervous/Worried
Sad	Embarrassed
Angry	Confused
Frustrated	Sarcastic
Formal	Disgusted
Excited	Surprised
Tired/Sleepy	Joyful
Bored	Confident
Annoyed	Exasperated
Scared	Proud

Unit 7: Growing Up, Changing Rules, and Transition
Lesson 6: Scavenger Hunt

LESSON OBJECTIVES

1. Students will work in groups to complete the social skills scavenger hunt.
2. Students will demonstrate important social skills through the activities assigned.
3. Students will be able to personally reflect on these activities and their success with them independently.

RATIONALE

This is a great culminating project for middle school students to engage in at the end of the year. It encompasses so many of the different social skills that have been worked on, and it is an opportunity for students to put their skills to the test in an authentic setting. Students at the middle school level thrive on different and unique opportunities, so taking students to an authentic setting, such as the mall, to practice social skills is an exciting opportunity for all. Working in groups, peer coaches assist students with prompting on achieving these challenges and practicing social skills. This scavenger hunt was created by our high school PEERspective class, so it also creates a rapport among the two groups and allows students to see the importance of the tasks since it is coming from an older population.

LESSON OVERVIEW AND INSTRUCTION

Lesson Duration

One to two 45-minute periods

Lesson Materials

- Scavenger hunt checklist
- Writing utensil
- Mall or outdoor shopping center

Lesson Activity

1. Students are taken to a mall or outdoor area where they can accomplish the social skills tasks provided on the scavenger hunt checklist; you may modify the checklist for your student population and the specific stores/amenities available to you.
2. Students work in groups to navigate the authentic setting and complete and document the tasks given.

> Social Emotional Learning Competencies (CASEL, 2020) addressed in this lesson:
>
> - Self-Awareness
> - Self-Management
> - Responsible Decision-Making
> - Relationship Skills
> - Social Awareness

Students enjoy part of their scavenger hunt challenge by practicing ordering at a restaurant and completing other social skill tasks.

We're Going on a Scavenger Hunt!

Group Names: _____

Required Scavenger Hunt Tasks:

1. Take a picture of another student posing like a mannequin.
2. Take a selfie with a store clerk.
3. Ask a clerk a question about the store or the products they sell.
4. Take a picture of a group member introducing themselves to someone and explaining what our field trip is about.
5. Take a picture of each of your group members going into a store they've never been to.
6. Take a picture in front of _____.
7. Take a picture of two group members high-fiving in _____.
8. Take a picture of a few group members in a conga line on the sidewalk.
9. Ask the book store if they have the book *Yes, Please Tell Me* by Jen Schmidt and Megan Barrett.
10. Take a picture of the food that you order.

_____/10 Points

Extra Time? BONUS!

11. Take a picture by _____
12. Take a picture of the majority of your members doing a grass angel.
13. Take a picture with any of the adult chaperones; 1 point per adult!

Bonus Points Total: _____

Unit 7: Growing Up, Changing Rules, and Transition Additional Activities and Ideas

- **Scavenger Hunt:** If your district has a middle and high school version of the PEERspective class, consider having the high school class design the middle school scavenger hunt and/or vice versa. This is a fun way to build rapport, create mentoring opportunities, and have age-appropriate tasks created by other young adults. The scavenger hunt in this unit was created originally by the high school class of 2019 for our middle school students!

- **Student-created videos:** As mentioned above, you can give students different scenarios and have them create a video script where they display the incorrect way to react to a problem, or maybe the way they would have reacted as a younger child, followed by a reaction that is more appropriate for a middle school student. After recording the videos, you can then have a film day—with popcorn, of course. Students love watching themselves and their classmates in action, and they start to see some behaviors they may exhibit and how other people react to that type of behavior. This can also be an opportunity to ask the students to present to the class and set up the scene prior to viewing the video they created.

- **Games:** When you are playing the games as a family, please be sure to prompt the students to do the following:

  1. Wait their turn
  2. Use eye contact when speaking to another person
  3. Use good sportsmanship (congratulate the winner, use positive language, keep a good attitude, and don't get upset if they don't win)

- **Student Debates:** Debates are the ultimate test when it comes to filtering thoughts, perspective-taking, and a multitude of other social skills. This can be a final exam or assessment to determine how the students are doing on these topics and should be completed toward the end of PEERspective. You can make this more fun by choosing silly topics like "Is a hot dog a sandwich?" The students think this is funny, and it can help to avoid some of the emotion surrounding controversial issues. This also alleviates the problem of who is correct because, well, there is no real answer to this question! Debates are especially effective for teaching perspective-taking because in order to prepare for a debate, you must consider the arguments that the opposing side will use.

- **Restaurant Etiquette:** This is another activity that would be great in an authentic setting if at all possible! Students can prepare for a restaurant outing by practicing restaurant etiquette in class with discussions about manners and tipping (i.e., why we socially expect customers to tip). Students can go over these rules and create visuals, then finally put their skills to the test with an actual outing at a restaurant. If it is not possible for your school to get students out to a food establishment, create your own in conjunction with your cafeteria and have a mock restaurant lunch at school!

Teacher name:
Teacher email:
Week of:

Parent Corner
Unit 7

Growing Up, Changing Rules, and Transition

We covered the following concepts in Unit 7:

- **Rules change with age.**
- Filtering your thoughts and feelings doesn't make you dishonest, it makes you **socially smart**.
- People have thoughts and feelings in their heads all day long that they don't share with others.
- It is vital to use a filter and ask yourself, **"Is it kind? Is it necessary? Can it wait until another time?"**
- Everyone looks at situations differently (has different perspectives) based on their past experiences and the information that is given to them. Often arguments are just **misunderstandings** based on a person's **perspective.**
- Emotions are not good or bad. It is okay to feel sad or angry.

Next steps at home:

- Remind your child as situations arise that rules change with age and to filter their thoughts using the three questions, "Is it kind? Is it necessary? Can it wait until another time?"
- If you feel comfortable, you can share with your child when you are filtering your thoughts and feelings to model the behavior. For example, "I was actually frustrated that our food took so long to get here, but I didn't say anything because I know the server is doing her best."
- Ask your child's teacher for a copy of the Awareness Matters Social Map used in PEERspective class. This could become a tool you use at home to help your child see other people's points of view on any given situation. You can also draw it yourself:

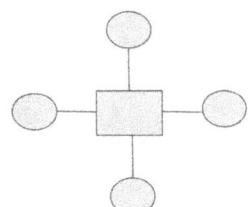 Write the situation in the middle rectangle and each person's potential perspective in the surrounding circles. If you are drawing this visual, you can add as many circles as you need. Remember, you are not necessarily trying to convince your child they are wrong; you are just creating awareness of others' perspectives.

- If your child is upset or angry, help them realize that it is normal to feel this way sometimes. You can help them find a coping strategy, or you can simply validate their feelings by saying something like, "I see you are upset and that is understandable. Let me know how I can help."

Thank you for supporting PEERspective! By using the same vocabulary and reinforcing what is being taught, you will help your child generalize these skills much more effectively. Please don't hesitate to contact me at the above email if I can support you or your child in any way!

UNIT 8

"WE GET TO WATCH A MOVIE?"

Using Film and Video Clips to Teach Social Skills

After the PEERspective program began in 2007, word spread among parents of students with special needs, and I was asked to do a class for students with more significant disabilities. I, of course, was more than happy to adjust what was being done with the students with mild autism to help a wider scope of students with multiple disabilities. I thought it would be "so easy" to just differentiate the lessons for a lower-ability class. Well, how wrong I was (again). I have taught high school students for the bulk of my career, and although I studied elementary education, I found it challenging at best to find materials that were age-appropriate, kept students' interest, and taught the content at the students' level. Inspired by one particular student who had a special interest in Disney movies, I tried using Disney movie clips to teach social skills, and I'm so glad I did! It worked like a charm. The students didn't even realize they were learning. Plus, if you choose a film they will watch multiple times (which they often do), it reinforces the skills/concepts taught through an evidence-based practice called video modeling!

"If you can't beat 'em, join 'em." In these technology-driven days, when seemingly every student has a smartphone, educators are in a constant battle to keep students engaged. Much has been written about the effect of screen time on students' ability to focus. Add the diagnosed attention or learning challenges faced by many of our students, and it can be even more difficult to keep students motivated and on task. Instead of trying to fend off the advances of technology, perhaps educators would find more success if we didn't try to beat them, but joined them—and video modeling is one way to do so.

Video modeling is simply using video or film to teach a new skill; this is a great strategy for all exceptionalities and grade levels and works for teaching a variety of skills. Video is especially useful when teaching social skills because it's much easier to see other people's social mistakes than to recognize and admit our own. Film and video clips also give you the option of freezing the character on the screen, allowing close inspection of nonverbal communication, including facial expressions and body language. Animated videos often feature exaggerated representations of social interactions, and animated characters' facial expressions are always elaborate, thus easy to interpret.

Video modeling is one of 27 evidence-based practices for students on the autism spectrum. Students with autism who typically struggle with communication and social skills have the greatest difficulty interpreting *nonverbal* communication. Given that so much of communication is nonverbal, these students can miss a lot of information! By using films and short video clips, educators and therapists can provide social intervention, teaching such skills as reading body language, perspective-taking, and even simpler tasks like starting a conversation or making eye contact.

First, educators and therapists should decide which social skill(s) they want to teach the students. From there, creating a lesson is as easy as previewing the clip or movie and identifying the skill you would like to illustrate. For example, if you are teaching the importance of self-regulation, you could try using *The Angry Birds Movie* or *Inside Out*. Working on dancing skills before a school dance? Use a clip from the movie *Hitch*, where the social coach in the film gives the important advice to "keep it at home" when you dance. Really, he is simply teaching the other character that in order to blend in, dance moves should be small and controlled—unless you can pull off "the sprinkler" dance move, which most of our students cannot. Video modeling can also be more personalized, reflecting your own students or school setting. If you want to reinforce students walking in an orderly line to the cafeteria, capture them in that positive behavior and play it back for them (Schmidt, 2020a).

This unit includes several film studies you can use throughout the year. We recommend using one film study per quarter, so the students don't ask you every day if they are going to watch a movie! If it's not possible to watch a movie in class, these activities could also be provided to families and done at home as an extension of your classroom work. The films included in this unit are ones our students have really enjoyed, but these preferences can change from year to year. Pay close attention to the needs of your students and ensure that they do not consider animated films too childish. Most middle and high school students, and even adults, enjoy animation, but using a film and format most popular with your current students is important. We have found that students enjoy these film studies and pick up on nonverbals such as facial expressions more easily when they are overly dramatized, which animation does well. In this unit, clips of popular TV shows are also provided; it is recommended that you use clips without animation throughout the year, as well.

Film studies allow you to freeze a particular part of the movie to evaluate facial expressions and other nonverbal cues. It is very effective to show students particular facial expressions and talk about what they might mean. I have even shown clips without sound (lesson found in *Why Didn't They Just Say That?* [Schmidt, 2017]) and asked the students to guess what was happening in the scene based on only nonverbals. Of course, this only works if the students are unfamiliar with that movie, show, or commercial.

We all know that as soon as the students realize you are showing a video clip, their interest is piqued, so for that reason alone, video modeling can work. Creating buy-in and teaching through modeling or demonstration are effective teaching strategies for *all* learners. Don´t believe it? When was the last time something broke in your house and you searched YouTube for a tutorial to fix it rather than calling someone? Yes, that's right—even you and I use video modeling.

Before we jump into the specific film studies, here are a few tips for success:

1. The film studies require that the entire film is viewed over multiple days for about 20 minutes a day if shown in school. The ideas covered during those 20 minutes are discussed prior to viewing, after viewing, and sometimes even during; be sure to tell students ahead of time that you'll be stopping it to discuss during the viewing, or you might have a revolt on your hands!

    o Throughout the film studies, consider pausing and discussing when appropriate to dissect the facial expressions of the main character and the reaction of the other characters. This is a helpful tool for teaching perspective-taking. Often our students don't realize that other people have thoughts and feelings based on our words and actions, and using film can help students grasp this concept because they can actually see the reactions.

2. If your students have average to above-average cognitive abilities, you could have them work in pairs or small groups to create their own film study based on various concepts you have taught throughout the year. This will encourage them to watch a movie and work on a project outside of class, applying what they learned. You can then use these film studies in the future.

3. Be sure to use non-animated clips throughout the school year as well. Consider your current students' preferences when deciding what videos to use from year to year.

4. At the end of a film study, we ask students to recommend a film to be studied next in social communication class. This is a great opportunity to get input from students about what movies they enjoy and create buy-in; it also gets the students to start thinking about social themes whenever they watch a movie for leisure. Sneaky, right?

Specific lessons include:

- *Inside Out* film study
- *A Bug's Life* film study
- *Toy Story 3* film study
- *The Angry Birds Movie* film study
- Social skills video clip mini-lessons

Answer keys to all film studies are provided in Appendix 10.

Unit 8: Using Film and Video Clips to Teach Social Skills
Lesson 1: Film Study

LESSON OBJECTIVES

1. Students will watch 20 minutes of the film each day.
2. Each student will work on answering the film study questions by themselves for 10 minutes.
3. Students will then work in pairs to complete the film study questions and discuss their initial thoughts/answers.
4. The class will discuss the answers to the film study questions.

RATIONALE

Film studies are a strategy used to help students build social awareness and read nonverbal communication more accurately in those around them. By using animated films in particular, facial expressions (especially eye contact) can be evaluated more easily. This format is effective because it's easier to pick out a social mistake that someone else is making rather than recognizing it in yourself. In order to correct a social mistake, the first step is awareness, and often students do not realize how their social interactions are perceived by those around them. Although animated films are not used exclusively, the benefit of using animated films is that the expressions and situations are generally exaggerated, making the social mistakes easier to find and the nonverbals easier to read. After deciding if these films are a good fit for your class, it is important to explain to them why you are using animated films. Finally, with film clips, the teacher can stop/freeze a scene and discuss the facial expressions, nonverbals, and different perspectives. In PEERspective, film studies often reinforce previous learning, so the questions tie in to what has been taught previously in class.

LESSON OVERVIEW AND INSTRUCTION

Lesson Duration

Three or four 45-minute class periods per movie

Lesson Materials

- Movie of your choosing
- Device to show movie
- Film study handout

Lesson Activity

1. In these lessons, students will view approximately 20 minutes of the film each day, then answer questions on the film study handout. These questions will guide the discussion between partners and then flow into a whole-class discussion, which allows the students to have more confidence and a trial run before sharing in front of a larger class.

Social Emotional Learning Competencies (CASEL, 2020) addressed in this lesson:

- Self-Awareness
- Self-Management
- Responsible Decision-Making
- Relationship Skills
- Social Awareness

Inside Out Film Study

Key concepts:

- We all have emotions
- Emotions are not "good" or "bad"
- It is normal to have joy, sadness, fear, disgust, or anger at times throughout your day
- Empathy is caring about what others think and feel
- We leave people with feelings (good, bad, or neutral) based on what we say and do
- Zones of Regulation (Kuypers & Winner, 2019)
- Above and Below the Line behavior (People Leaders, 2019)
- Using a greeting and a closing in conversations
- Friendship and how to be a good friend
- Trust and why it's so important not to break trust

(Del Carmen, 2015)

Inside Out Film Study

Name _____ Date _____

Day #1, 0–20 minutes

Write about your initial thoughts on watching *Inside Out*.

1. Riley has many different emotions. These emotions are Joy, Sadness, Fear, Disgust, and
   _____.

2. When Riley's dad is feeding her broccoli, Anger gets very mad. What Zone is Riley in?
   _____

3. When Riley saw her new house, she felt _____.

   You can tell because: _____

4. It is _____ for Riley to be feeling a lot of different emotions about moving.

If I had to move, I'd feel _____. Why?

Inside Out Film Study

Name_____ Date_____

Day #2, 21–40 minutes

1. After Riley cries in front of the class, she hides her head behind her history book because she is _____, showing her emotions not through her words but through what?

2. Riley becomes angry and is not nice to her dad. When people are not nice to others, the other people have _____ thoughts in their heads about them.

3. When people have negative thoughts about you, how do they treat you?
   _____

4. Riley yelling at her dad is ABOVE / BELOW the Line behavior. (circle one)

5. When Riley is talking to her friend from home, she becomes upset and interrupts her friend, saying that she needs to go. Is it nice to end a conversation with your friends like that? Yes/No

   How could she have said goodbye in a better way? _____

6. Joy starts a conversation with Bing Bong. What steps does she do well? _____

Inside Out Film Study

Name_____ Date_____

Day #3, 41–60 minutes

1. While playing hockey, Riley becomes very _____.

2. Why do you think she feels this way? _____

3. Sadness is being a good _____ to Bing Bong. What does Sadness do well?
   _____

4. Bing Bong, Joy, and Sadness are trying to wake Riley up for the _____ to start moving again.

What do you think about the movie so far? Who is your favorite character and why? Who is your least favorite character and why?

Inside Out Film Study

Name_____ Date_____

Day #4, 60 minutes–end

1. Joy tells Sadness that she had a good idea. Sadness has _____ thoughts about Joy in her head.

2. Why do you think she has these thoughts?
   _____

3. Riley decides to take money from her mom. This destroys _____ island.

4. Have you ever broken a parent's trust? Explain below.
   _____

5. Riley decides to run away from home. This is ABOVE / BELOW the Line behavior. (circle one)

6. Before jumping on the trampoline, Joy feels _____. You can tell because she
   _____

7. Joy and Sadness are working _____ to help Riley.

8. Would you recommend this movie to a friend? Why or why not?
   _____

Now it's your turn! Write a proposal below to suggest a movie you have enjoyed for our next film study! Explain why you are suggesting this movie and what social communication lessons we can learn from it.

If your movie is chosen as a top recommendation, you will be asked to present a short pitch (like a commercial) to your peers to convince them to vote for your movie choice.

A Bug's Life Film Study

Key concepts:

- Size of the problem (Winner, 2019)
- Zones of Regulation (Kuypers & Winner, 2019)

    1. How to determine the problem
    2. How to decide what Zone you are in
    3. How to use a coping strategy
    4. How to fix the problem
    5. How to stay in the Green Zone

- We can help other people stay calm if you stay calm
- We often mirror other people's emotions and feelings
- Being creative and unique is good
- Believe in yourself and your ideas, and don't let other people make you doubt yourself
- People have thoughts about you, and these thoughts can change over time based on your interactions with them
- Importance of friendship

(Anderson & Reher, 1998)

Please note: For this film study, time stamps are listed for each question instead of dividing the film into 20-minute increments. You can stop the film and have the students answer right away at each time stamp, or you can watch for 20 minutes and then have them answer the questions at the end if you prefer. Stopping the film at the given time stamp is a good way to modify this activity for students who may need a little help. This also allows the teacher to rewind and show scenes again if needed. This is mentioned in the "Tips and Tricks" section of this unit as a level 3 intervention.

Name: _____

A Bug's Life Film Study

1. What is the problem? (2:07)

   _____
   _____

2. How did the ant feel when the leaf fell? What Zone? (2:15)

   _____
   _____

3. How did the ants fix the problem? (2:24)

   _____
   _____

4. How did the ant feel when the problem was fixed? What Zone? (2:35)

   _____
   _____

5. What Zone is Princess Atta in? What Zone should she be in? (3:30)

   _____
   _____

6. What Zone is Flik in? Why? (6:00)

   _____
   _____

7. What is the problem? (9:50)

   _____
   _____.

8. Why is Flik special? (15:00)

   _____
   _____.

9. Are the bugs *actually* warriors? (30:00)

   _____
   _____.

10. What strategy did the bugs use? (32:00)

    a. Fidget spinner
    b. White lie
    c. Deep breaths
    d. Talking it out

11. Do the ants really think the bugs will kill the grasshoppers? (35:30)

    a. Yes
    b. No

12. Do the bugs plan on killing the grasshoppers? (35:30)

    a. Yes
    b. No

13. What Zone are the ants in? (36:30)

    _____
    _____.

14. What are the bugs noticing now? (39:00)

    _____
    _____.

15. What Zone is Flik in? (40:45)

   _____
   _____.

16. What strategy is Flik using to fix the problem? (47:40)

   a. White lie
   b. Talking it out
   b. Fidget spinner
   d. Deep breaths

17. How do Flik's decisions impact the ants' feelings? (1:02.00)

   _____
   _____.

18. How do the other bugs feel when Flik becomes happy? (1:09.50)

   _____
   _____.

19. What is Flik doing? (1:19.30)

   _____
   _____.

20. How did the ants feel about Flik at the beginning of the movie, and how do they feel about Flik at the end of the movie?

   _____
   _____.

21. Are princess Atta and Flik friends at the end of the movie?

   a. Yes
   b. No

22. What did Flik do to help the ant colony?

   _____
   _____.

Toy Story 3 **Film Study**

Key concepts:

- We all have emotions.
- Emotions are not "good" or "bad."
- It is normal for your interests to change as you get older.
- Teenagers and young adults outgrow playing with toys.
- Teenagers don't usually play with toys, especially in public.
- Empathy is the ability to share the feelings of others.
- It is important to show empathy toward other people you care about.
- A bully repeatedly intimidates or is mean to someone else.
- It is not nice to bully other people. We should treat others with kindness.
- People have bad thoughts about people who bully others.
- When someone is sad, you can tell because they are not smiling or engaging with others, and they may frown and not make eye contact.
- We have thoughts and feelings about others based on their words and actions. These feelings are good, bad, or neutral.
- When someone is surprised, their face shows it by having wide-open eyes and an open mouth.

(Anderson, 2010)

Toy Story 3 Film Study

Name_____ Date_____

Day #1, 0–20 minutes

Use the words below to fill in the following questions. Use each word only once:

empathy
scared
outgrew
normal
loved

1. As Jesse and Woody's train headed toward the broken bridge, they must have felt _____.

2. When Andy was little, he _____ his toys and played with them every day.

3. As Andy got older, he _____ his toys.

4. It is _____ for high school students to stop playing with toys.

5. When Woody tells the other toys it will be okay even though he doesn't really think it will, he is showing _____.

6. What do you think about the movie so far? Who is your favorite character and why?

_____

Toy Story 3 Film Study

Name_____ Date_____

Day #2, 21–40 minutes

Andy   crush

bad   bullied

Lotso   happy

1. At first the toys felt _____ about being at Sunny Side.

2. Barbie and Ken seem to have a _____ on each other. You can tell because they _____.

3. Woody wants to leave Sunny Side because he wants to stay with _____.

4. The toys now seem to feel _____ at Sunny Side.

5. _____ is being a bully.

6. When people are bullies, others have _____ thoughts in their heads about them.

Toy Story 3 **Film Study**

Name_____ Date_____

Day #3, 41–60 minutes

1. Bullseye seems very sad. He doesn't say he's sad, but you can tell because_____.
   _____

2. The children at Sunny Side play too rough with the toys. This makes the toys feel _____
   _____.

3. When Buzz hears what is really going on at Sunny Side he is _____.
   . (happy, nervous, sad)

4. When Mrs. Potato Head sees Andy looking for her and the other toys, she feels _____.
   (happy, anxious, sad)

5. When the toys are locked up, they fee _____.
   (excited, scared, worried)

Toy Story 3 Film Study

Name_____ Date_____

Day #4, 61–80 minutes

1. The clown has (circle one) **good / bad** feelings in his head about Lotso.

2. Lotso is very _____ (excited, happy, sad) about his owner leaving him.

3. Lotso **does / does not** show empathy to the other toys. He knows how it feels to be separated from your owner.

4. Woody looks really _____ (scared, happy, sad) when he gets back to Sunny Side and sees how the children are treating his friends.

5. The Phone **does / does not** show empathy when he helps Woody plan the big escape. He knows how it is to live in Sunny Side.

Toy Story 3 Film Study

Name_____ Date_____

Day #5, 81–108 minutes

1. The toys are _____ (sad, afraid, surprised) that Buzz is suddenly speaking Spanish.

2. Buzz likes Jesse. Even though he is speaking Spanish, you can tell he likes her because he _____ _____.

Draw a picture of one of your favorite scenes in this movie. Why did you choose this scene?

Angry Birds Film Study

Key concepts:

- Above and Below the Line behavior (Kuypers & Winner, 2019)
- Zones of Regulation (Kuypers & Winner, 2019)

    1. What are the Zones of Regulation, and how do you know which Zone you are in?
    2. How do you use coping strategies to get to the Green Zone?
    3. If you start to feel that you are in the Yellow or Red Zones, you should Stop, Opt, and Go!

- If you make a mistake, you should say you are sorry and try to make better choices.
- Before we say something, we should ask these three questions: Is it kind? Is it necessary? Can it wait until another time?
- We need to use a thought bubble and filter our thoughts by asking the three questions above *before* sharing what is in our heads.
- We should use different voice volumes for different situations.
    o Before the film study, read the picture book *Decibella and Her 6-Inch Voice* by Julia Cook (2014). If you can't get the book, you can find it read aloud on YouTube. In the book, the voice volumes are whisper, 6-inch, table talk, strong speaker, and outside voice. This is great information to use during the film study and in life!

(Cohen & Winder, 2016)

Angry Birds Film Study

Name_____ Date_____

Day #1, 0–20 minutes

1. What were your initial thoughts on watching *The Angry Birds Movie*? _____

2. The little green bird was using her _____ voice when yelling. Using the wrong voice volume is _____ behavior.

3. Red's choice when he shoved cake in the bird's face was _____ the Line. (Above or Below)

4. When Mr. Red says "Not a good joke" to the judge, he should have used his _____ bubble. A code word that we have learned to help us remember to keep an opinion to ourselves is _____.

5. Movement, such as yoga or dancing, is good to use as an option in the _____ Zone.

6. When Bomb blows up, he is in the Red Zone. Next time, he should stop, look at his _____, and go with the best one to calm down.

Angry Birds Film Study

Name_____ Date_____

Day #2, 20–40 minutes

1. Red feels _____ when others exclude him.

2. The therapy bird, Matilda, was in the Red Zone, so she picked the option of taking deep breaths to get back to the _____ Zone. What option do you usually use when you are in the Red Zone?

3. When the big red bird, Terrance, was upset that Red lied and blamed him, instead of Terrance punching him, he should have made a/an Above / Below (circle one) the Line choice.

4. It was an _____ behavior when Ross hugged someone without permission.

5. It is okay to use your _____ when cheering with others.

6. Red used his _____ voice when they were sneaking around the ship. Name a time when you should use this voice volume.

7. When was a time that you felt yourself in the Red Zone? Did you choose an option to help you get back to the Green Zone?

Angry Birds Film Study

Name_____ Date_____

Day #3, 40–60 minutes

1. Matilda, the therapist, was in the _____ Zone when she was feeling anxious and upset, so she used deep breaths to get back to the Green Zone. Name two things that make you anxious or upset. What coping strategies do you use to get back to the Green Zone?

2. Throwing the guitar was a/an Above / Below (circle one) the Line choice.

3. Mr. Red was disappointed with Mighty Eagle because he would not help him save the town. When was a time you were disappointed with someone, and did you make an Above the Line choice?
   _____

4. When the pigs take the eggs, they are _____, which is a Below the Line choice.

5. Insulting someone can make them _____ or sad.

Angry Birds Film Study

Name_____ Date_____

Day #4, 60–end

1. Since the town felt bad about being mean to Red, they should have said "I'm _____."

2. Matilda, the therapist, was in the Yellow Zone, so she stopped, looked at her _____, and went with the best choice of deep breaths.

3. It's important to cover your _____ when you sneeze.

4. When Clarence, the yellow bird, wrote "fart face," his choice was Above / Below (circle one) the Line.

5. Everyone was sad when they thought Red died. They were running slow, so they were in the _____ Zone.

6. The town made a/an Above / Below (circle one) the Line choice by fixing Red's house as an apology.

7. Slamming the door on someone is unacceptable even if you are in the _____ Zone. You need to stop, opt, and go!

8. When was a time you had to say sorry to someone? _____

Unit 8: Using Film and Video Clips to Teach Social Skills
Lesson 2: Social Skills Video Clip Mini-Lessons

LESSON OBJECTIVES

1. Students will watch the clip to identify targeted social skills.
2. Each student will work individually or in a pair as determined by the instructor.
3. At the end of class, students will discuss the takeaway of the lesson as it applies to social skills.

RATIONALE

Short video clips can clearly show a student what to do or what not to do. This is especially helpful when teaching perspective-taking and explaining that other people have thoughts and feelings about us based on our words and actions. It is much easier for students to pick out unexpected social behavior in someone else, especially in a video clip. After they see how this behavior may make others feel, they can see it in themselves more readily and are more motivated to change or eliminate the behavior.

With video clips and animated films, the expressions and situations are generally exaggerated, which makes them easier to find. Using films or video clips also allows the teacher to stop/freeze a scene to discuss or dissect the facial expression. In PEERspective, clips are used frequently to teach various skills as the need arises. Searching YouTube and keeping folders available for different social skills can make this an easy addition to your weekly lesson plans. Please see the "How to" guide to learn more about how to easily add videos to your PowerPoints or file them on YouTube. You can also challenge the students to find clips and create lessons (depending on their ability level and the internet filters at your school) as an extension activity. Finally, these clips are a fun and easy way to teach social skills remotely or virtually.

LESSON OVERVIEW AND INSTRUCTION

Lesson Duration

> One 45-minute class period

Lesson Materials

- Video clip of your choosing (see links following lesson)
- Device to show video

Lesson Activity

In this lesson, students will view a clip showing a specific social skill; the clip may show the desired behavior, or it could show what *not* to do. Video clips can help demonstrate a variety of skills such as skill acquisition, vocabulary or lesson reinforcement, social mistakes, and being more socially aware in your thinking.

Video clips for each of these areas have been provided in the "Video Links" folder, and your lesson plan can be created in a variety of ways. You may consider having the students journal once prior to showing the clip, and then again after in order to know where their knowledge is. You can use a peer coach and allow the pair to discuss the clip, and you can use these clips to teach students individually or even remotely. (They're also ideal for speech therapy sessions.)

Social Emotional Learning Competencies (CASEL, 2020) addressed in this lesson:

- Self-Awareness
- Self-Management
- Responsible Decision-Making
- Relationship Skills
- Social Awareness

Lesson Outline Video Reference Links

Nonverbal Communication Video Links
Glee nonverbals:
https://www.youtube.com/watch?v=bWdyHMAtNMk
These short clips from the TV show *Glee* are compiled together and can be used to show nonverbal communication. The overdramatization in so many of these offers ample opportunities to pause and dissect facial expressions and other nonverbal communication.

Positive nonverbal communication:
https://www.youtube.com/watch?v=5lqhMRi2yE4
In this movie clip from the 2021 *Tom & Jerry* film, Tom uses hand gestures to communicate to the main human character, Kayla Forrester, by blowing them up like a balloon and twisting them to make the name "Tom." Because he cannot speak or sing, this is the best way for him to let people know his name. It allows them to better understand what he is saying.

Negative nonverbal communication:
https://www.youtube.com/watch?v=N7lGqmZprx0
This retail worker makes the customer feel uncomfortable because of the way he is speaking. Everything he is saying can be interpreted differently based on the gestures he uses.

"Gestures":
https://www.youtube.com/watch?v=0cIo0PkBs2c
This video is a guide for using gestures so that people can effectively communicate nonverbally. This will help students learn what to look for when speaking and listening nonverbally.

Friends video:
https://www.youtube.com/watch?v=OvEci5Bjgd4
This video from the TV show *Friends* demonstrates various examples of how you can show emotion through nonverbal communication. In most of these scenarios, the actors use their facial expressions to communicate what they are thinking.

Social "Don'ts" Video Links
Double dip the chip:
https://www.youtube.com/watch?v=RfprRZQxWps&list=PLFdAe7oxp6ewHoUGBTgBLi__F2eREY5J9&index=4
This *Seinfeld* clip shows the etiquette rule of only dipping your chip into dip once; watching it can lead to a lesson on other social etiquette rules and what people may think if you break them. You can discuss that although these rules are not posted anywhere, in society it is important to know and follow them, especially in public. A possible follow-up lesson is how the rules can change based on where you are and who you're with; in other words, we may act differently at home than we do in school or at a restaurant.

iCarly:
https://www.youtube.com/watch?v=CxsKwn9SlVY
In this *iCarly* clip, Sam is hungry when leaving her date, so she takes a burger out of the trash and starts eating it.

Studio C dinner party:
https://www.youtube.com/watch?v=pjF8QZPgUKk
In this Studio C comedy sketch, there are a few examples of what should be done on a date, and a lot of examples of what people should NOT do on a date.

Big Bang Theory:
https://www.youtube.com/watch?v=3_dAkDsBQyk
In this clip, Sheldon is showing a social "don't" by not listening to the conversation.

The Office:
https://www.youtube.com/watch?v=K1KEo99yOOc
In this clip, Oscar is trying to talk with Pam and Toby at their book club, and Phyllis is trying to heat up her popcorn. She is completely interrupting Oscar's conversation by pushing hundreds of buttons, and Oscar finally has had enough.

Disgusting Krabby Patty:
https://www.youtube.com/watch?v=koGemCchmpQ
In this clip from S*pongeBob SquarePants*, a rotten Krabby Patty that was found under the grill of the Krusty Krab kitchen is served to a customer. Due to its appearance and smell, it causes the restaurant to be devoid of customers. It is unhealthy to serve a customer rotten food, regardless of how much money that would save. That could result in the health department shutting the restaurant down, putting SpongeBob, Squidward, and Mr. Krabs out of a job. Later, Mr. Krabs eats the patty and gets sick. Eventually, the patty gets surgically removed from Mr. Krabs's skin and he ends up rethinking his choices.

Parks and Recreation:
https://www.youtube.com/watch?v=TUTAL9LDHRc
In this clip, Ron Swanson has called the entire Parks department to gather around the coffee pot, which is broken. Ron asks if anyone knows who broke it. The Parks department proceeds to blame each other until it escalates to incoherent yelling. At the end of the clip, Ron reveals that he was the one who broke the coffee pot, and that he just told everyone that it was broken to cause chaos.

Victorious:
https://www.youtube.com/watch?v=NfkEbiHlAng
This video compiles many times when Sinjin tries to "flirt" with or really just speak to Jade, but instead he comes off creepy and obnoxious. He repeatedly tries to make comments about them being together. As a result, it is weird and awkward for them and everyone around them.

Big Bang Theory:
https://youtu.be/Na3QDHzJcxs
This video shows Sheldon continuously knocking on Penny's door and not picking up on the hints that he is not wanted at her door.

Kicking & Screaming:
https://youtube/Ozpkzjl-oCU:
In this movie clip, Will Farrell's character gets impatient at a coffee shop, and instead of respectfully leaving or asking to speed up the line, he starts yelling. He then proceeds to forget the owner's name, which will create an even worse impression than he had already made.

Restaurant Etiquette Video Links
Soup slurper:
https://www.youtube.com/watch?v=unXKYK0uRJ8&list=PLFdAe7oxp6ewHoUGBTgBLi__F2eREY5J9&index=2
This *King of Queens* clip shows annoying sounds that should be avoided when eating with other people. This can also be used to illustrate nonverbal reactions to a dining faux pas and the importance of being aware of people around you and their thoughts and feelings.

Table Manners 101: Basic Dining Etiquette:
https://www.youtube.com/watch?v=FDGGv7z5r2c
This clip is an informational video about basic table manners that you can show prior to a class social outing that includes dining out.

Restaurant Etiquette:
https://youtu.be/bROOWTpyTlg
This amusing clip demonstrates dining etiquette and table manners.

Steps to Use Clips to Teach Social Skills: A How-To Guide

During a recent webinar, a participant asked me a great question: Is there an online resource library to find good video clips? I have had a lot of luck simply searching YouTube. Now that my school uses Chromebooks, I've found it even easier to input these clips into Google Slides. I have listed the steps below for you. It's pretty straightforward, and once you begin using the clips, your students will start to give you recommendations.

1. Open a Google Slides presentation.
2. Go to Insert on the toolbar.
3. Select Video.
4. YouTube will automatically come up. Search here or in a separate tab.
5. Type a movie, TV show, or skill you want to find (Example: "Hitch dancing").
6. Insert the clip into your slide and watch it. You can go back and edit it later if it's longer than you'd like, or you can just take note of where to start and stop the video.

When following the steps above, you cannot watch the clip until it is in Slides, so it may be easier to open another tab, search YouTube, and then go back and insert the clip once you've found the one you are certain you'd like to use.

Another way to make it easy to incorporate clips into your lessons is to create easy-to-access videos on a playlist. Adding videos from YouTube into your own watchlist is an easy and effective way to quickly access the clips that you want to share with your students in order to teach a concept. In order to do this, you should follow the following steps:

1. Go to YouTube.com.
2. Sign in to your account.
3. Choose the video that you want to save to your playlist.
4. Underneath the video, there will be a button that says "save."
5. You will then be given a choice to add the video to an existing playlist or to create a new playlist.
6. Your video will then be added to your chosen playlist for you to reference whenever needed.

REFERENCES

Alberto, P. A., Cihak, D. F., & Gama, R. I. (2005). Use of static picture prompts versus video modeling during simulation instruction. *Research in Developmental Disabilities, 26*(4), 327–339. https://doi.org/10.1016/j.ridd.2004.11.002

Alwell, M., & Cobb, B. (2009). A map of the intervention literature in secondary special education transition. *Career Development for Exceptional Individuals, 29*(1), 3–27. https://doi.org/10.1177%2F08857288060290010301

American Psychiatric Association. (2013). Diagnostic and statistical manual of mental disorders (5th ed.). https://doi.org/10.1176/appi.books.9780890425596

Anderson, D.K. (Producer), & Unkrich, L. (Director). (2010). *Toy story 3* [Film]. United States: Pixar Animation Studios.

Anderson, D.K. & Reher, K. (Producer), & Lasseter, J. (Director). (1998). *A bug's life* [Film]. United States: Pixar Animation Studios.

Apple, A. L., Billingsley, F., & Schwartz, I. S. (2005). Effects of video modeling alone and with self-management on compliment-giving behaviors of children with high-functioning ASD. *Journal of Positive Behavior Interventions, 7*(1), 33–46. https://doi.org/10.1177%2F10983007050070010401

Bandura, A. (1977a). Self-efficacy: Toward a unifying theory of behavioral change. *Psychological Review, 84*(2), 191–215. https://psycnet.apa.org/doi/10.1037/0033-295X.84.2.191

Bandura, A. (1977b). *Social learning theory*. Upper Saddle River, NJ: Prentice Hall.

Bandura, A. (1993). Perceived self-efficacy in cognitive development and functioning. *Educational Psychologist, 28*(2), 117–148. https://doi.org/10.1207/s15326985ep2802_3

Baron-Cohen, S., Tager-Flusberg, H., & Lombardo, M. (Eds.). (2013). *Understanding other minds: Perspectives from developmental social neuroscience*. Oxford University Press. https://doi.org/10.1093/acprof:oso/9780199692972.001.0001

Bass, J. D., & Mulick, J. A. (2007). Social play skill enhancement of children with autism using peers and siblings as therapists. *Psychology in the School, 44*(7), 727–734. https://doi.org/10.1002/pits.20261

Bates, P. E., Cuvo, T., Miner, C. A., & Korabeck, C. A. (2001). Simulated and community-based instruction involving persons with mild and moderate mental retardation. *Research in Developmental Disabilities, 22*(2), 95–115. https://doi.org/10.1016/S0891-4222(01)00060-9

Bellini, S. (2006). *Building social relationships: A systematic approach to teaching social interaction skills to children and adolescents with autism spectrum disorders and other social difficulties.* Shawnee Mission, KS: Autism Asperger Publishing Co.

Bellini, S., Peters, J., Brenner, L., & Hopf, A. (2007). A meta-analysis of school-based social skills interventions for children with autism spectrum disorders. *Remedial and Special Education, 28*(3), 153–162. https://doi.org/10.1177%2F07419325070280030401

Center on the Developing Child. (n.d.). *Executive function and self-regulation.* Harvard University. https://developingchild.harvard.edu/science/key-concepts/executive-function/

Cdaughe. (2018, April 1). Great book for motivated teachers working with ASD students - I think it could also be used for summer "homemade" activities. [Review of *Why Didn't They Just Say That*, by J. Schmidt]. Retrieved from https://www.amazon.com/gp/customer-reviews/R265AISUYH1HFP/ref=cm_cr_arp_d_rvw_ttl?ie=UTF8&ASIN=1942197349

Cihak, D., Alberto, P. A., Taber-Doughty, T., & Gama, R. I. (2006). A comparison of static picture prompting and video prompting simulation strategies using group instructional procedures. *Focus on Autism and Other Developmental Disabilities, 21*(2), 89–99. https://doi.org/10.1177%2F10883576060210020601

Cohen, J. & Winder, C. (Producers), & Kaytis, C. & Reilly, F. (Directors). (2016). *The angry birds movie* [Film]. United States: Columbia Pictures.

Collaborative for Academic, Social, and Emotional Learning (CASEL). (2020, December). *SEL: What are the core competence areas and where are they promoted?* CASEL. https://casel.org/core-competencies/

Cook, J. (2014). *Decibella and her 6 inch voice.* Boys Town: Boys Town Press.

Crabtree, C. (Host). (2020, August 7). *Back to school panic* [Audio podcast]. https://podcasts.apple.com/us/podcast/back-to-school-panic/id1233384453?i=1000487385500

Crooke, P., & Winner, M. G. (2011). *Social fortune, or social fate: A social thinking® graphic novel map for social quest seekers: Watch their destiny unfold based on the choices they make.* San Jose, CA: Social Thinking Publishing.

Del Carmen, R. (Producer) & Docter, P. (Director). (2015) *Inside Out* [Film]. Pixar Animation Studios.

Denham, S., Mason, T., Caverly, S., Schmidt, M., Hackney, R., Caswell, C., & Demulder, E. (2001). Preschoolers at play: Cosocializers of emotional and social competence. *International Journal of Behavioral Development, 25*(4), 290–301. https://doi.org/10.1080%2F016502501143000067

Eaves, L. C., & Ho, H. H. (2008). Young adult outcome of autism spectrum disorders. *Journal of Autism and Developmental Disorders, 38*, 739–747. https://doi.org/10.1007/s10803-007-0441-x

Endow, J. (2016, August 2). *Autism, social greetings and rhetorical questions.* http://www.judyendow.com/autistic-behavior/autism-social-greetings-and-rhetorical-questions/

Fenaughty, J. (2014). *Game-based strategies implementation during social skills training for non-elementary aged individuals* (Doctoral dissertation, University of Central Florida). UCF's Showcase of Text, Archives, Research & Scholarship. http://stars.library.ucf.edu/cgi/viewcontent.cgi?article=5532&context=etd

Folkman, Z. (2013). *Zenger Folkman research uncovers how to not get fired* [Press release]. http://www.prnewswire.com/news-releases/zenger-folkman-research-uncovers-how-to-not-get-fired-225040792.html

Ganz, J., Heath, A., Lund, E., Camargo, S., Rispoli, M., Boles, M., & Plaisance, L. (2012). Effects of Peer-based implementation of visual scripts in middle school. *Behavior Modification, 36*(3), 378–398. https://doi.org/10.1177%2F0145445512442214

Gillott, A., Furniss, F., & Walter, A. (2001). Anxiety in high-functioning children with autism. *Autism, 5*(3), 277–286. https://doi.org/10.1177/1362361301005003005

Gresham, F. M., Sugai, G., & Horner, R. H. (2001). Interpreting outcomes of social skills training for students with high-incidence disabilities. *Teaching Exceptional Children, 67*(3), 331–344. https://doi.org/10.1177%2F001440290106700303

Hart, K. J., & Morgan, J. R. (1993). *Cognitive behavior procedures with children and adolescents: A practical guide.* Boston, MA: Allyn Bacon.

Hebron, J., & Humphrey, N. (2014). Exposure to bullying among students with autism spectrum conditions: A multi-informant analysis of risk and protective factors. *Autism, 18*(6), 618–630. https://doi.org/10.1177%2F1362361313495965

Humphrey, N., & Symes, W. (2010). Perceptions of social support and experiences of bullying among pupils with autism spectrum disorders (ASD) in mainstream secondary schools. *European Journal of Special Needs Education, 25*(1), 77–91. https://doi.org/10.1080/08856250903450855

Iovannone, R., Dunlap, G., Huber, H., & Kincaid, D. (2003). Effective educational practices for students with autism spectrum disorders. *Focus on Autism and Other Developmental Disabilities, 18*(3), 150–165. https://doi.org/10.1177/10883576030180030301

Kientz, M. A., & Dunn, W. (1997). A comparison of the performance of children with and without autism on the sensory profile. *American Journal of Occupational Therapy, 51*, 530–537. https://doi.org/10.5014/ajot.51.7.530

Koul, R. K., Schlosser, R. W., & Sancibrian, S. (2001). Effects of symbol, referent, and instructional variables on the acquisition of aided and unaided symbols by individuals with autism spectrum disorders. *Focus on Autism and Other Developmental Disabilities, 16*(3), 162–169. https://doi.org/10.1177%2F108835760101600304

Kuypers, L. M., & Winner, M. G. (2019). *The zones of regulation: A curriculum designed to foster self-regulation and emotional control.* Santa Clara, CA: Think Social Publishing, Inc.

Lang, S. (2018). *The grumpy monkey.* New York: Random House Children's Books.

Laushey, K. M., & Heflin, L. J. (2000). Enhancing social skills of kindergarten children with autism through the training of multiple peers as tutors. *Journal of Autism and Developmental Disorders, 30*, 183–193. https://doi.org/10.1023/A:1005558101038

March, J., & Mulle, K. (1998). *OCD in children and adolescents: A cognitive behavioral treatment manual.* New York, NY: Guilford Press.

Marzano, R. J. (2012, October 1). Art and science of teaching/The many uses of exit slips. *Students Who Challenge Us, 70*(2), 80–81. ASCD. http://www.ascd.org/publications/educational-leadership/oct12/vol70/num02/The-Many-Uses-of-Exit-Slips.aspx

Merrell, K. W., & Gimpel, G. A. (1998). *Social skills of children and adolescents: Conceptualization, assessment, treatment.* Mahwah, NJ: Lawrence Erlbaum Associates.

Moss, H. (2010). *Middle school: The stuff nobody tells you about.* Shawnee Mission, KS: AAPC.

Myles, B. S., Trautman, M., & Schelvan, R. L. (2013). *The hidden curriculum: For understanding unstated rules in social situations for adolescents and young adults.* Future Horizons.

Myles, B. S., Mahler, K., & Robbins, L. (2016). *Sensory issues and high-functioning autism and related disorders. Practical solutions for making sense of the world.* Shawnee Mission, KS: AAPC Publishing.

Myles, B. S., & Simpson, R. L. (2001). Understanding the hidden curriculum: An essential social skill for children and youth with Asperger Syndrome. *Intervention in School and Clinic, 36*(5), 279–286. https://doi.org/10.1177%2F105345120103600504

National Geographic Kids. (n.d.). *The first Thanksgiving: Native Americans and early settlers gave thanks together with this historic feast.* https://kids.nationalgeographic.com/history/article/first-thanksgiving

Neneng, H., & Suherdi, D. (2017). The effectiveness of jigsaw in improving students' reading comprehension. *Journal of English and Education, 5*(1), 1–12. https://ejournal.upi.edu/index.php/L-E/article/view/9895

Odom, S., L., McConnell, S. R., & McEvoy, M. A. (1992). *Social competence of young children with disabilities: Issues and strategies for intervention*. Baltimore, MD: Paul H. Brookes.

Ohio Department of Education. (n.d.). Each child, our future: Ohio strategic plan for education 2019–2024. http://education.ohio.gov/About/EachChildOurFuture

National Parent Center on Transition and Employment. (2012). *Skills to pay the bills*. Pacer.org. https://www.pacer.org/transition/video/series.asp?se=39

People Leaders. (n.d.). *Where do you sit? Above or below the line?* https://peopleleaders.com.au/above-or-below-the-line/

Pierce, M. (2018, October). *Is it okay to lie?* Scholastic Scope. https://scope.scholastic.com/issues/2018-19/100118/Is-It-OK-to-Lie.html

Quinn, M. M., Kavale, K. A., Mathur, S. R., Rutherford Jr., R. B., & Forness, S. R. (1999). A meta-analysis of social skills interventions for students with emotional and behavioral disorders. *Journal of Emotional and Behavioral Disorders, 7*(1), 54–64. https://doi.org/10.1177%2F106342669900700106

Radley, K. C., Roderick, D. O., Ness, E. J., Ford, W. B., Battaglia, A. A., McHugh, M. B., & McLemore, C. E. (2014). Promoting social skill use and generalization in children with autism spectrum disorder. *Research in Autism Spectrum Disorders, 8*(6), 669–680. https://doi.org/10.1016/j.rasd.2014.03.012

Rao, P., Beidel, D., & Murray, M. (2008). Social skills interventions for children with Asperger's Syndrome and high-functioning autism: A review and recommendations. *Journal of Autism and Developmental Disorders, 38*, 353–361. https://doi.org/10.1007/s10803-007-0402-4

Reaven, J., & Hepburn, S. (2003). Cognitive-behavioral treatment of obsessive-compulsive disorder in a child with Asperger syndrome. *Autism, 7*(2), 145–164. https://doi.org/10.1177%2F1362361303007002003

Risch, N., Hoffman, T. J., Anderson, M., Croen, L. A., Grether, J. K., & Windham, G. C. (2014). Familial recurrence of autism spectrum disorder: Evaluating genetic and environmental contributions. *The American Journal of Psychiatry, 171*(11), 1206–1213. https://doi.org/10.1176/appi.ajp.2014.13101359

Rivera, J. (Producer), & Docter, P. (Director). (2015). *Inside out* [Film]. United States: Pixar Animation Studios.

Sasso, G. M., Mundschenk, N. A., Melloy, K. J., & Casey, S. D. (1998). A comparison of the effects of organismic and setting variables on the social interaction behavior of children with developmental disabilities and autism. *Focus on Autism and Other Developmental Disabilities, 13*(1), 2–16. https://doi.org/10.1177%2F108835769801300101

Schmidt, J. M. (2017). *"Why didn't they just say that?": Teaching secondary students with high-functioning autism to decode the social world using PEERspective: an evidence-based practice: Peer-based instruction and intervention*. Future Horizons.

Schmidt, J.M. (2020a). *Using film to teach social skills to students with unique learning needs*. N2yblog. https://www.n2y.com/blog/using-film-to-teach-social-skills/

Schmidt, J.M. (2020b). *Easy, fun ways to help children stay social while at home.* N2yblog. https://www.n2y.com/blog/stay-social-while-at-home/

Schmidt, J.M. (2020c). *How to help my autistic child cope with quarantine.* AAPC Publishing Blog. https://www.aapcautismbooks.com/a/blog/how-to-help-my-autistic-child-cope-with-quarantine

Scully, K. (2017, October 1). *Games to improve executive functioning skills.* Pathway2Success. https://www.thepathway2success.com/games-to-improve-executive-functioning-skills/

Seaman, A. M. (2012, September 3). *Almost half of teens with autism bullied: Study.* Chicago Tribune. http://articles.chicagotribune.com/2012-09-03/lifestyle/sns-rt-us-teen-autismbre8820lg-20120903_1_autism-spectrum-disorder-asperger-autistic-children

Sherman, J., Rasmussen, C., & Baydala, L. (2008). The impact of teacher factors and behavioral outcomes for children with attention deficit/hyperactivity disorder (ADHD): A review of the literature. *Educational Research, 50*(4), 347-360. https://doi.org/10.1080/00131880802499803

Steinbrenner, J. R., Hume, K., Odom, S. L., Morin, K. L., Nowell, S. W., Tomaszewski, B., Szendrey, S., McIntyre, N. S., Yücesoy-Özkan, S., & Savage, M. N. (2020). Evidence-based practices for children, youth, and young adults with Autism. The University of North Carolina at Chapel Hill, Frank Porter Graham Child Development Institute, National Clearinghouse on Autism Evidence and Practice Review Team. https://fpg.unc.edu/publications/evidence-based-practices-children-youth-and-young-adults-autism-spectrum-disorder-1

Stichter, J. P., Conroy, M. A., & Kauffman, J. M. (2007). *An introduction to students with high incidence disabilities*. Upper Saddle River, NJ: Prentice Hall.

Stichter, J. P., O'Connor, K. V., Herzog, M. J., Lierheimer, K., & McGhee, S. D. (2012). Social competence intervention for elementary students with Asperger's Syndrome and high functioning autism. *Journal of Autism and Developmental Disorders, 42*, 354-366. https://doi.org/10.1007/s10803-011-1249-2

Stichter, J. P., Randolph, J., Gage, N., & Schmidt, C. (2007). A review of recommended social competency programs for students with autism spectrum disorders. *Exceptionality, 15*(4), 219–232. https://doi.org/10.1080/09362830701655758

Strain, P. S., & Odom, S. L. (1986). Peer social initiations: An effective intervention for social skill deficits of preschool handicapped children. *Exceptional Children, 52*(6), 543–552. https://doi.org/10.1177%2F001440298605200607

Tirado, M. (2018, September 13). *The Wampanoag side of the first Thanksgiving story.* Indian Country Today. https://indiancountrytoday.com/archive/the-wampanoag-side-of-the-first-thanksgiving-story

Wagner, T. (2008). *The global achievement gap*. New York, NY: Basic Books.

Wilkins, S., & Burmeister, C. A. (2015). *Flipp the switch: Strengthen executive function skills.* Future Horizons.

Winner, M.G. (2018, September 18). *Social thinking: Thinking with your eyes.* [Webinar]. Think Social Publishing, Inc. https://www.socialthinking.com/eLearning/Webinar-Thinking-With-Your-Eyes

Winner, M. G. (2019, April 10). *Social thinking: Size of the problem.* [Webinar]. Think Social Publishing, Inc. https://www.socialthinking.com/eLearning/Webinar-Size-of-Problem

Winner, M. G., & Crooke, P. (2011). *Socially curious and curiously social: A social thinking guidebook for bright teens & young adults.* Santa Clara, CA: Think Social Publishing.

Wong, C., Odom, S. L., Hume, K. A., Cox, C. W., Fettig, A., Kurcharczyk, S., et al. (2015). Evidence-based practices for children, youth, and young adults with autism spectrum disorder: A comprehensive review. *Journal of Autism and Developmental Disorders, 45*, 1951-1966. https://doi.org/10.1007/s10803-014-2351-z

Yakubova, G., & Taber-Doughty, T. (2013). Effects of video modeling and prompting on social skills embedded within a purchasing activity for students with autism. *Journal of Special Education Technology, 28*(1), 35–47. https://doi.org/10.1177%2F016264341302800104

Yeager, D. S., & Dweck, C. S. (2012). Mindsets that promote resilience: When students believe that personal characteristics can be developed. *Educational Psychologist, 47*(4), 302–314. https://doi.org/10.1080/00461520.2012.722805

Zablotsky B., Bradshaw, C.P., Anderson, C.M., & Law, P. (2014) Risk factors for bullying among children with autism spectrum disorders. *Autism, 18*(4), 419–427. https://doi.org/10.1177%2F1362361313477920

Zernike, K. (2010, November 20). *The pilgrims were … socialists?* New York Times. https://www.nytimes.com/2010/11/21/weekinreview/21zernike.html

APPENDICES

Appendix 1

Autism Social Skills Profile-2

Scott Bellini, Ph.D., HSPP
Indiana University, Bloomington

```
Child's Name_____
                     First                                                                    Last
Birthdate_____ Age_____ Sex ☐Female ☐Male Today's Date_____
           Month Day Year                                              Month    Day    Year
School_____Grade_____
                                          City
Your Name_____

Relationship to Child  ☐Mother ☐Father ☐Guardian ☐Other _____

Street Address_____

City_____State_____Zip_____Phone_(____)_____
```

The following phrases describe skills or behaviors that your child might exhibit during social interactions or in social situations. Please rate **HOW OFTEN** your child exhibits each skill or behavior independently, **WITHOUT ASSISTANCE FROM OTHERS** (i.e., without reminders, cueing and/or prompting). You should base your judgment on your child's behavior over the last **9 weeks**.

Please use the following guidelines to rate your child's behavior:

Circle **N** if your child **never** or **almost never** exhibits the skill or behavior.

Circle **S** if your child **sometimes** or **occasionally** exhibits the skill or behavior.

Circle **O** if your child **often** or **typically** exhibits the skill or behavior.

Circle **V** if your child **very often** or **always** exhibits the skill or behavior.

Please do not skip any items. If you are unsure of an item, please provide your best estimate. You may use the "with prompting" section to indicate whether the particular skill can be performed with additional assistance from adults. For instance, if your child will exhibit a particular skill or behavior more frequently when cueing or prompting is provided, or when interacting with adults rather than peers, please place an "X" in the "with prompting" section. Please use the "Additional Information" section at the end of the rating scale to provide additional information on the child's social skills and social cognitive functioning.

Bellini's Autism Social Skills Profile-2

Component Skill	How Often?				With Prompting?	Scoring			
						SER	SPA	DSB	Total
Invites peers to join him/her in activities	N 1	S 2	O 3	V 4		▓		▓	
Joins in activities with peers	N 1	S 2	O 3	V 4		▓		▓	
Takes turns during games and activities	N 1	S 2	O 3	V 4			▓	▓	
Interacts with peers during unstructured activities	N 1	S 2	O 3	V 4		▓		▓	
Asks questions about a broad range of topics	N 1	S 2	O 3	V 4		▓	▓		
Asks questions to request information about a person	N 1	S 2	O 3	V 4			▓		
Engages in one-on-one social interactions with peers	N 1	S 2	O 3	V 4		▓	▓		
Interacts with groups of peers	N 1	S 2	O 3	V 4		▓			
Maintains the "give and take" of conversations	N 1	S 2	O 3	V 4			▓		
Talks about or acknowledges the interests of others	N 1	S 2	O 3	V 4			▓		
Exhibits poor timing with his/her social initiations	N 4	S 3	O 2	V 1		▓	▓		
Page 2 scoring summary						SER	SPA	DSB	Total

Bellini's Autism Social Skills Profile-2 *(continued)*

Component Skill	How Often?				With Prompting?	Scoring			
						SER	SPA	DSB	Total
Changes the topic of conversation to fit self interests	N 4	S 3	O 2	V 1		▓	▓		
Recognizes the facial expressions of others	N 1	S 2	O 3	V 4			▓	▓	
Adjusts voice volume based on the needs of the listener	N 1	S 2	O 3	V 4		▓	▓	▓	
Recognizes the non-verbal cues, or "body language" of others	N 1	S 2	O 3	V 4			▓	▓	
Understands the jokes or humor of others	N 1	S 2	O 3	V 4			▓	▓	
Maintains an appropriate distance when interacting with peers	N 1	S 2	O 3	V 4		▓	▓		
Considers the viewpoints of others in social situations	N 1	S 2	O 3	V 4			▓		
Engages in socially inappropriate behaviors	N 4	S 3	O 2	V 1		▓	▓	▓	
Verbally expresses how he/she is feeling	N 1	S 2	O 3	V 4		▓		▓	
Allows peers to join him/her in activities	N 1	S 2	O 3	V 4		▓		▓	
Joins a group conversation by politely interrupting or waiting for a pause/break in conversation	N 1	S 2	O 3	V 4			▓	▓	
Engages in solitary interests and hobbies	N 4	S 3	O 2	V 1				▓	
Expresses sympathy for others when they are hurt or upset	N 1	S 2	O 3	V 4		▓	▓	▓	
Page 3 scoring summary						SER	SPA	DSB	Total

Bellini's Autism Social Skills Profile-2 *(continued)*

Component Skill	How Often?				With Prompting?	Scoring			
						SER	SPA	DSB	Total
Experiences negative peer interactions	N 4	S 3	O 2	V 1		▓	▓		
Initiates greetings with others	N 1	S 2	O 3	V 4			▓	▓	
Says "sorry" or apologizes for mistakes	N 1	S 2	O 3	V 4		▓	▓	▓	
Provides compliments to others	N 1	S 2	O 3	V 4		▓	▓	▓	
Acknowledges the compliments directed at him/her by others	N 1	S 2	O 3	V 4			▓	▓	
Responds to the invitations of peers to join them in activities	N 1	S 2	O 3	V 4		▓		▓	
Responds to questions directed at him/her by others	N 1	S 2	O 3	V 4			▓	▓	
Experiences positive peer interactions	N 1	S 2	O 3	V 4		▓			
Compromises during disagreements with others	N 1	S 2	O 3	V 4		▓	▓	▓	
Misinterprets the intentions of others	N 4	S 3	O 2	V 1		▓	▓		
Offers assistance to others	N 1	S 2	O 3	V 4			▓	▓	
Uses gestures or eye contact to direct the attention of others to objects, persons, or situations	N 1	S 2	O 3	V 4		▓	▓	▓	
Ends conversations abruptly	N 4	S 3	O 2	V 1		▓	▓		
Page 4 scoring summary						SER	SPA	DSB	Total

Bellini's Autism Social Skills Profile-2 *(continued)*

Component Skill	How Often?	With Prompting?	Scoring			
			SER	SPA	DSB	Total
Fails to read cues to terminate conversations	N S O V 4 3 2 1		▓	▓		
Introduces self to others	N S O V 1 2 3 4			▓	▓	
Exhibits fear or anxiety regarding social interactions	N S O V 4 3 2 1		▓		▓	
Is manipulated by peers	N S O V 4 3 2 1		▓			
Engages in solitary activities in the presence of peers	N S O V 4 3 2 1		▓		▓	
Interacts with peers during structured activities	N S O V 1 2 3 4		▓		▓	
Makes eye contact when initiating interactions with others	N S O V 1 2 3 4		▓	▓	▓	
Maintains appropriate levels of eye contact during conversations	N S O V 1 2 3 4		▓	▓	▓	
Responds to the greetings of others	N S O V 1 2 3 4			▓		
Successfully adapts behavior to new settings and situations	N S O V 1 2 3 4		▓	▓	▓	
Says "excuse me" or politely asks others to move out of his/her way	N S O V 1 2 3 4			▓	▓	
Makes inappropriate comments	N S O V 4 3 2 1		▓	▓		
Page 5 scoring summary			SER	SPA	DSB	Total

Please provide additional information on the child's social skills and social cognitive functioning:

_____
_____
_____
_____
_____
_____
_____
_____
_____
_____

ASSP-2 Scoring Summary

	SER	SPA	DSB	TOTAL
Page 2				
Page 3				
Page 4				
Page 5				
	SER Total	SPA Total	DSB Total	ASSP TOTAL

STANDARD SCORE _____

PERCENTILE RANK _____

Autism Social Skills Profile-2
Total Raw Score to Standard Score Conversion Table*
High Functioning ASD**

Raw Score	Standard Score	Percentile Rank	Raw Score	Standard Score	Percentile Rank	Raw Score	Standard Score	Percentile Rank
49	53	<1	91	86	18	133	118	88
50	54	<1	92	87	19	134	118	88
51	55	<1	93	87	19	135	119	90
52	56	<1	94	88	21	136	120	91
53	57	<1	95	88	21	137	121	92
54	57	<1	96	89	23	138	122	93
55	57	<1	97	90	25	139	123	94
56	58	<1	98	91	27	140	123	94
57	59	<1	99	92	30	141	124	95
58	60	<1	100	93	32	142	125	95
59	61	<1	101	94	34	143	126	96
60	62	1	102	94	34	144	127	96
61	63	1	103	95	37	145	128	97
62	64	1	104	96	40	146	129	97
63	64	1	105	97	42	147	129	97
64	65	1	106	98	45	148	130	98
65	67	1	107	99	47	149	130	98
66	68	2	108	99	47	150	131	98
67	68	2	109	100	50	152	132	98
68	69	2	110	100	50	153	132	98
69	69	2	111	101	53	154	133	99
70	70	2	112	101	53	155	134	99
71	71	3	113	101	53	156	135	99
72	72	3	114	102	55	157	136	99
73	72	3	115	103	58	158	136	99
74	72	3	116	104	61	159	137	99
75	73	4	117	105	63	160	138	99
76	74	4	118	106	66	161	139	>99
77	75	5	119	107	68	162	140	>99
78	76	5	120	108	70	163	141	>99
79	77	6	121	109	73	164	142	>99
80	78	7	122	110	75	165	143	>99
81	78	7	123	110	75	166	144	>99
82	79	8	124	111	77	167	144	>99
83	80	9	125	112	79	168	145	>99
84	81	10	126	113	81	169	145	>99
85	82	12	127	114	82	170	146	>99
86	83	13	128	114	82	171	147	>99
87	84	14	129	115	84	172	147	>99
88	84	14	130	116	86	173	148	>99
89	85	16	131	116	86	174	149	>99
90	85	16	132	117	87	>174	>150	>99

*Standard Scores have a mean of 100, and a Standard Deviation of 15. Normative data are based on parent reports only.

Table is used with youth on the autism spectrum, ages 6-17, who do **not have a cognitive disability or significant language impairment

Autism Social Skills Profile-2
Total Raw Score to Standard Score Conversion Table*
Non Verbal or Cognitive Disability **

Raw Score	Standard Score	Percentile Rank	Raw Score	Standard Score	Percentile Rank	Raw Score	Standard Score	Percentile Rank
49	<50	<1	91	94	34	133	139	>99
50	50	<1	92	95	37	134	140	>99
51	51	<1	93	96	40	135	142	>99
52	52	<1	94	97	42	136	143	>99
53	53	<1	95	98	45	137	144	>99
54	54	<1	96	99	47	138	145	>99
55	55	<1	97	100	50	139	146	>99
56	55	<1	98	101	53	140	147	>99
57	56	<1	99	102	55	141	148	>99
58	57	<1	100	103	58	142	149	>99
59	58	<1	101	105	63	143	150	>99
60	59	<1	102	106	66	144	>150	>99
61	61	<1	103	107	68	145	>150	>99
62	63	1	104	108	70	146	>150	>99
63	63	1	105	109	73	147	>150	>99
64	64	1	106	110	75	148	>150	>99
65	65	1	107	111	77	149	>150	>99
66	68	2	108	112	79	150	>150	>99
67	69	2	109	113	81	152	>150	>99
68	69	2	110	114	82	153	>150	>99
69	70	2	111	115	84	154	>150	>99
70	71	3	112	116	86	155	>150	>99
71	72	3	113	117	87	156	>150	>99
72	72	3	114	118	88	157	>150	>99
73	73	4	115	119	90	158	>150	>99
74	75	5	116	120	91	159	>150	>99
75	76	5	117	121	92	160	>150	>99
76	77	6	118	123	94	161	>150	>99
77	78	7	119	124	95	162	>150	>99
78	79	8	120	125	95	163	>150	>99
79	81	10	121	126	96	164	>150	>99
80	83	13	122	128	97	165	>150	>99
81	84	14	123	129	97	166	>150	>99
82	84	14	124	130	98	167	>150	>99
83	85	16	125	131	98	168	>150	>99
84	86	18	126	132	98	169	>150	>99
85	87	19	127	132	98	170	>150	>99
86	88	21	128	133	99	171	>150	>99
87	89	23	129	134	99	172	>150	>99
88	90	25	130	135	99	173	>150	>99
89	91	27	131	136	99	174	>150	>99
90	93	32	132	137	99	175	>150	>99

*Standard Scores have a mean of 100, and a Standard Deviation of 15. Normative data are based on parent reports only.

**Table is used with youth on the autism spectrum, ages 6-17, who have a cognitive disability or significant language impairment

Appendix 2

Sample Proposal to Administration

PEERspective

This proposal is to teach a yearlong class to students with social skill deficits at the middle school level. Completion of this class will count as an elective credit for students.

Rationale

We have many students with social communication deficits in our school. Many have been diagnosed with autism or social communication disorder. Some of these students have IEPs for speech-language services, as well as tutoring from a special educator. At times, they do not work as well as their peers in groups when assigned to participate with others on a collaborative assignment. Many of these students eat alone at lunch and do not socialize as well as their peers. Finally, these students often are targets for bullying or unknowingly make inappropriate comments at school that get them into trouble.

Units

Unit 1 – Friendship, Rapport Building, and Trust
Unit 2 – Anticipated Middle School Behaviors
Unit 3 – Dealing with Setbacks and Change
Unit 4 – Executive Functioning
Unit 5 – Using a Filter and Thinking Socially
Unit 6 – Navigating Social Media in Middle School
Unit 7 – Growing Up, Changing Rules, and Transition
Unit 8 – Using Film and Video Clips to Teach Social Skills

Class Structure

The class will be made up of targeted students with social skill deficits and trained peer coaches who will participate in class alongside the targeted students. The class will consist of:

1. Instruction
2. Discussion
3. Practice/role-play
4. Social games to practice skills
5. Film studies
6. Projects and other activities to practice working as a group and making friends using appropriate socialization skills
7. Field trips/outings to practice skills in authentic middle school settings

Appendix 3

Middle School PEERspective Syllabus

Dear Students and Parents,

It is my pleasure to have the opportunity to work with you this year! I **KNOW** it's going to be a fantastic year!

I have put together the following information to let you know about my classroom procedures and expectations. I encourage students and parents to read through the information together so that everyone is familiar with the policies and procedures for the year. Parents and students, please sign the bottom portion of this page and return it to me by _____ so that I know you both have reviewed the material.

Please do not hesitate to contact me with any questions or concerns. I would also encourage you to visit our district's grade program to help keep up with student assignments and grades.

Sincerely,

_____

I have read and understand all listed classroom guidelines and protocols.

Student Signature:

_____

Parent Signature:

_____

Social Communication Class

Teacher's name: Room number: Email:

Course Description/Purpose

This course provides students with an understanding of human behavior. Interpersonal skill development is incorporated to help students recognize and enhance skills that are essential for building and maintaining relationships. To develop these skills, students are encouraged to share their ideas, thoughts, and feelings with their peers, as well as to participate in group-interaction activities in authentic settings. Each quarter we will have a field trip and outside activity to further explore topics discussed in class. These activities give students the chance to practice socializing in appropriate ways. In order to meet these goals, students must enhance the interpersonal skills that are essential for building and maintaining relationships, including trust, communication, acceptance, and conflict resolution.

Course Topics

- Friendship, Rapport Building, and Trust
- Anticipated Middle School Behaviors
- Dealing with Setbacks and Change
- Executive Functioning
- Using a Filter and Thinking Socially
- Social Media in Middle School
- Growing Up, Changing Rules, and Transition

Teacher Responsibilities

I will treat each student as a young adult and with respect. Respect goes both ways, so we will learn and share with each other throughout the year. I will assess assignments in a timely manner. I will also return parent phone calls and emails within 24 hours. I am here to help students succeed in the classroom and to be an advocate whenever needed. You EARN your own grade.

Requirements for Student Assignments

- *Attendance and Participation:* This course is based on building interpersonal skills, so it is important to come to class and participate regularly. Most of your grade will be based on participation in group activities and discussions; therefore, absences will severely hurt your grade.
- *Required Items:* You should bring these items to class each day: Pen or pencil, notebook for journal assignments, required student text

Grading Policies

The school's grading scale will be used. Adding the total number of points earned and dividing that by the total number of points possible will average your grades.

TOTAL EARNED/TOTAL POSSIBLE= PERCENTAGE GRADE

Plagiarism and copying of any kind will result in the following discipline procedures that align with school and district policy:

First offense: Student will earn a 0 on the assignment and parent/guardian will be notified.

Second offense: Student will earn a 0 on the assignment and two detentions, a parent conference will be held with an administrator, and a discipline referral will be kept on file.

Third offense: Students will earn a 0 on the assignment, a parent conference will be held with an administrator, and the student will be assigned Saturday School or suspension. Also, the grade for that quarter will be lowered by one letter grade (11%).

Classroom Procedures

1. When a school announcement is made: If an announcement of any kind is made during class, you are to immediately stop what you are doing and listen, even if you do not believe the announcement applies to you.

2. Entering class: Please enter our room at voice level 0–1 (inside/whisper), and take your seat immediately. If you need something, get it and be back in your seat when the bell rings. Also, please keep your hands and body to yourself and set up your work area. When the bell rings, you are expected to be at a level 0 and be working.

3. Supplies: Handle these needs before the bell rings. Borrow what you need, or see the student supply shelf. It's expected that you regularly bring all the supplies you need—including a pencil! See me if you need help with this.

4. Tardiness: Class starts immediately. You'll have your card marked if you're not in your seat when the bell rings.

5. Process for beginning work: Your desk should be clear of everything but the materials needed for THIS class; nothing personal or from another class needs to be on your desk. Be sure to read and follow directions.

6. Cell phones and other school rules: We will faithfully abide by the school rules.

7. Sharpening pencils (and other individual needs): DO THIS BEFORE THE BELL RINGS, PLEASE!

8. Absence: If you are absent from class, it's your responsibility to find out the information and work that you missed. After checking with your classmates, you may come to me for any needed materials to make up assignments.

9. Speaking: When requesting to answer a question, please raise your hand and do not speak until you are called on. Please be aware that all students have the right to participate and the need to share "airspace" as equally as possible. I appreciate your enthusiasm! But please be aware of how much and how often you speak so that you do not dominate the discussions. Also, please raise your hand to participate when you can, as a quiet room with no participation is not beneficial to your learning and understanding of concepts.

10. Listening: Listen closely to others as they speak. It's called *active listening* and is a learned skill. Remain open-minded, and if you're arguing a point, imagine and think through the other person's point of view.

11. Partner/group work: First, turn to face one another and stay seated and with your group. Talk with your group *only*, and limit your conversation to the topic you have been asked to work on. Do your fair share.

12. Courtesy: This means be considerate and helpful to all in our room. Examples: let another go first, say "please," "thank you," "excuse me," and "sorry." Everyone, including you, has the right to be respected!

13. Moving around: Personal space is yours. General space is ours. Please keep all parts of you and your belongings out of others' personal space, and we'll do the same for you. And please help keep all areas of the room clean and picked up.

14. Pass usage: Once permission is granted from the teacher, the student must completely fill out the plastic hall pass before leaving the room.

15. Moving to and from lunch, library, and other areas: Voice level 0; respect other students' learning.

16. Visitors/observers in class: Visitors to our classroom will be in and out. Some will stay awhile, and others will be quick. Do your best to keep your mind on what we're doing.

17. Dismissal: Please wait for your teacher to dismiss you. The class will be dismissed when the room is in order and all students are in their seats and silent.

Appendix 4

Sample Form for Teachers to Complete to Identify Potential Student Participants

PEERspective Data Collection Sheet

Student's Name _____ Date_____

Evaluator _____

During the observed class period please track the number of times each below behavior occurs:

_____ Joins in the activity with his/her peers without prompting

_____ Maintains eye contact when speaking or listening

_____ Speaks with appropriate volume in conversations

_____ Initiates greetings with others

_____ Maintains appropriate distance when interacting with others

_____ Considers others' opinions

_____ Stays on topic

_____ Smiles at peers/teacher at appropriate times

\# of times above behaviors were demonstrated in a _____ minute group activity

= _____

Anecdotal Summary of Observation

From Schmidt, J. Why didn't they just say that? Teaching secondary students with high-functioning autism to decode the social world using PEERspective. Future Horizons. ©2018. Used with permission.

Appendix 5

Sample Letter to Parents of Targeted Students

Dear Parents,

Your child has been chosen to be part of a middle school social communication class based on the PEERspective Learning Approach. This is a social skills course with a special focus on communication. While taking this course, your child will learn social skills needed to communicate more effectively. Your child has been chosen because he/she could benefit from intentional social skill training. The topics we will cover include trust and team building, anticipated middle school behaviors, accepting ourselves and others, executive functioning, dealing with setbacks and change, social media etiquette, and life transitions.

With your permission, the counselors will adjust your child's schedule to include this class. Your child will be expected to participate in all assignments and activities. The class will include peer coaches who have been hand-selected and trained to be social models while taking the course.

Please sign the attached page and return it to me as soon as possible. If you have any specific questions at this time, please feel free to contact me. I look forward to working with your child next year!

Sincerely,

Teacher:

School:

Phone number:

Parent email: _____

(Return this page)

Please include my child, _____, in the social communication class for the upcoming school year. I understand that the counselor will adjust my child's schedule to reflect this placement.

Parent Signature _____ Date: _____

Appendix 6

Sample Letter to Parents of Potential Peer Coaches

Dear Parents,

Your child has been recommended by their teacher(s) to be a peer coach for next year's social communication class, which is based on the PEERspective Learning Approach. This class will cover a social skills curriculum with a special focus on communication skills. While taking this course, your child will serve as a social role model for other students who are learning to communicate more effectively. Although your child is serving as a peer model, all students will participate in the class and earn a grade.

Some of the students in the class struggle with everyday communication in social situations. A lot of the students with communications needs have high functioning autism and are in general or advanced classes. Your child has been chosen because he/she exhibits strong social skills, character, and empathy, and works easily with a variety of students. Each of our peer coaches has been hand-selected for this important role. Many have already worked with their peers with communication difficulties and have shown great compassion and patience, and the class would not be as effective without their participation.

We will hold a required peer coach training session for all middle school peer coaches over the summer. This session will cover characteristics of autism and social communication needs and will train the students to be effective peer coaches. Failure to attend the training without advance notice will result in dropping this class.

Please fill out the bottom portion and return it to (teacher's name) by (due date).

_____

Please include my child, _____, as a peer coach. I understand that this class may take the place of another elective class.

Parent Signature _____ Date: _____

Peer Coach Agreement

I am interested in being a peer coach for Social Communication Class. I am willing to attend the training session over the summer. I understand that I will be taking the course for a grade, as well as coaching my peers on effective communication strategies.

Student Signature _____ Date: _____

Appendix 7

Peer Coach Training Agenda

Training presentations, agenda, and videos are available in the *Yes, Please Tell Me!* Google Drive.

9:00–9:30 a.m.: Getting to Know You activity

9:30–10:00 a.m.: KWL Chart: What you **K**now, what you **W**ant to know, and what you've **L**earned about autism (complete K and W here)

10:00–11:00 a.m.: Presentation: Autism training

11:00–11:15 a.m.: Simulation Game: How does it feel to have autism?

11:15–11:30 a.m.: Targeted student, past peer coaches, and parent videos and discussion

11:30–12:30 p.m.: Lunch

12:30–1:00 p.m.: Presentation: How to become a successful peer coach

1:00–2:00 p.m.: Wrap-up (KWL chart, complete the L, and make sure all the "want to know" questions were answered), answer any other questions

Appendix 8

E-Learning/Homeschool Tools

This resource, found on the following pages, was created in conjunction with Rilie McKaig, SLP, and was originally published on n2y using SymbolStix Prime (Schmidt, 2020b).

LEVEL 1

MONDAY
Problem Solving

You want to go outside but it is raining. What should you wear?

A Coat and gloves

B Rain jacket and boots

C Flip flops and a swimsuit

💬 You can make this a yes/no question by giving the scenario and then asking, "Should you wear ___? Yes or no?"

TUESDAY
Perspective Shifting

Your mom asked you to bring your dish to the sink, and you didn't do it.

This makes your mom feel ___.

A Sad

B Happy

C Angry

💬 Put the above words on notecards. Consider adding facial cues. It becomes can help guide your child's hand to point to the answer they think is best.

WEDNESDAY
Body Language

You feel happy when your mom picks you up from school. When you see your mom pulling up to your school you should ___ so she knows you are happy to see her.

A Frown

B Smile

C Cry

Practice using the appropriate facial expression and identifying it when you feel different ways throughout the week.

💬 Make this a yes/no questions by stating the scenario and then asking, "Should if you frown when you feel happy?" "Should you smile when you feel happy?" "Should you cry when you feel happy?"

THURSDAY
Figurative Language

Draw a picture of what it means when someone says it is "raining cats and dogs."

The next time it's raining hard, be sure to use this metaphor!

💬 This can be a fun activity to do with your child – consider drawing letters by and then figuratively.

FRIDAY
Functional Skills

What is the day of the week?

A Monday

B Tuesday

C Friday

What is the month?

A February

B May

C July

What is the day of the month?

A 2

B 12

C 22

What is the year?

A 1997

B 2020

C 2041

💬 You can make these yes/no questions by asking the questions and stating each option: "Is today the ___? Yes or no?"

💬 These comments are for parents or caregivers.

LEVEL 2

MONDAY Problem Solving	TUESDAY Perspective Shifting	WEDNESDAY Body Language	THURSDAY Figurative Language	FRIDAY Functional Skills
You forgot your homework at home and it is due today. How can you solve this problem?	Identify five perspectives of others in the following scenario: You have been given multiple assignments to complete for school, but you have not turned any of them in.	Make a video using iMovie or YouTube showing correct body language in a conversation and one video using incorrect body language. Share your video with one friend or person in your home.	Identify whether there is sarcasm in the following examples: • You heard a friend complaining about a mistake her mom made, and you said, "Wow! Well, it's a good thing you're perfect." • You're about to start a class assignment and your teacher says, "If you need help, please raise your hand."	Think about one chore you can do around the house to help a family member and do it without them asking for your help.
You are in a new school, and you are not sure where to sit at lunch. You see many people sitting and talking, and you don't know where you belong. There are some people from your math class that you recognize near the back wall. Where should you sit or what should you do?	Identify the perspective from the following people involved: You and your parents, teacher, classmates and friend.	Discuss and/or show what your eyes do when you are surprised.	Discuss how to use the following similes or metaphors: • Your bedroom is clean as a whistle. • I am your shining star. • His eyes were like ice as he stared at her.	Determine three questions you can ask yourself that will help you filter your thoughts. Doing so will help you choose the best time and place to share your thoughts!
	Write down three different perspectives of others for the following social situation:	Discuss and/or show what your hands do when you feel angry.		
	Your mom made dinner but you did not like the food. When you took your first bite you put your fork down and exclaimed, "Ew, how can you expect me to eat THIS?"	Discuss and/or show what your mouth does when you feel happy.		
		Discuss and/or show what you look for to know how someone is feeling.		

APPENDICES

ALL LEVELS

Movies

MONDAY Problem Solving	TUESDAY Perspective Shifting	WEDNESDAY Body Language	THURSDAY Figurative Language	FRIDAY Functional Skills
FINDING NEMO How did Nemo solve his problem of being separated from his dad? How would you have handled being lost and away from your family?	A BUG'S LIFE Discuss with those in your home how the bugs in town changed their minds about Flik from the beginning of the movie to the end.	TANGLED When Rapunzel escapes from the castle she experiences many emotions. List 3–5 of them. You may need to rewind this scene and watch it more than once!	FROZEN / FROZEN II Discuss a time when Olaf used figurative language in one of the Frozen movies with someone in your home.	INSIDE OUT Name the five emotion characters. Think about a time when you experienced one of these emotions. Which character are you feeling most like today? Why?

Games

① Please be sure to prompt your child to 1) wait their turn, 2) make eye contact when speaking to another person and 3) use good sportsmanship (e.g. they should congratulate the winners, use positive language, keep a good attitude and not get upset if they don't win).

MONDAY Problem Solving	TUESDAY Perspective Shifting	WEDNESDAY Body Language	THURSDAY Figurative Language	FRIDAY Functional Skills
OLD MAID CLUE (HIGHER LEVEL) ① These games provide two different levels of problem solving and can be played by the whole family.	APPLES TO APPLES (FAMILY EDITION) ① In this game the "Judge" chooses which card they like. The other players must think about the "judge" would pick, which may or may not be what the player likes. Be sure that you use the family edition.	FACE IT ① Each person makes a face that acts out something written on the card, and then tries to reveal it to another person while trying not to laugh. Be sure the cards are appropriate for the age and ability of the game guests. This game is designed for teens and adults but can be modified for younger students.	BLURT ① This game helps develop vocabulary. Each player listens to a definition and guesses the vocabulary word. For example, "hard, grainy, is a rock."	PICTIONARY ① In this game you draw a word without talking or giving clues. You can create this game at home with materials supplies if you prefer not to purchase the game set.

243

Appendix 9

Social Communication Bingo

Home School/E-learning

Level 1

Play a board game with a member of your family.	Offer to help your parent(s) with a chore.	Ask your parent(s) to tell a story about when you were a little kid.	Call a family member and talk to them on the phone.	Ask someone in your house if they'd like to watch a movie with you.
Make "Above the Line" choices all day long	Talk to your parents or a friend about a situation that is a "Can't Control."	Give someone in your family a compliment.	Smile and wave at a neighbor when you are outside.	Text a friend something positive like, "I hope you are doing okay. I miss you."
Call a friend or family member and tell them what you've been doing with your time lately.	Write a letter to your parents about what you are thankful for.	**FREE SPACE**	Write a positive sign to put up in your window for people walking outside.	Email a teacher something positive.
Tell your parents how you are doing today. Are you feeling happy, sad, or in between?	Tell someone in your family about a friend from school.	Tell someone in your family a funny story that happened at school this year.	Ask someone in your family if they want to listen to your favorite song.	Call a friend and ask them something like, "What have you been up to?"
Ask a family member if they want to go on a short walk in your neighborhood.	Write a list of 5 small talk topics you could talk to most people about (for example, the weather).	Ask your parents if you can help make dinner.	Tell someone in your family a funny joke.	Share with a family member what your favorite subject in school is and explain why.

Appendix 10

Film Study Answer Keys

Inside Out Film Study Answer Key

Day #1:

1. Anger
2. Red Zone
3. Sad, she looked down, frowned, and slumped her shoulders
4. natural/normal

Day #2:

1. Embarrassed, her facial expressions and nonverbals
2. Negative
3. Usually when people have negative thoughts about you, they don't want to spend time with you and may treat you in a less friendly way.
4. Below
5. No, she should have used a white lie and a less abrupt closing.
6. She used a greeting.

Day #3:

1. Frustrated
2. She missed the goal and became sad about moving and having to try out for a new team.
3. Friend, Sadness shows empathy and tries to Bing Bong.
4. Train

Day #4:

1. Good
2. Because she is trying to help her.
3. Honesty
4. [answers will vary]
5. Below
6. Nervous. She was using positive self-talk to help overcome her fears.
7. Together
8. [answers will vary]

A Bug's Life Film Study Answer Key

1. The leaf fell in the middle of the line, and the ant is unsure what to do.
2. He felt scared and confused.
3. The head ant guided the ant back into the line.
4. They felt relieved. They were in the Green Zone.
5. Princess is in the Yellow Zone. She is worried and on high alert. She should be in the Green Zone.
6. Flik is in the Yellow Zone. He is excited and extremely loud.
7. Flik's invention knocks off all of the food offering that the ants had been collecting.
8. He tried to stop Hopper from messing with Dot. He is allowed to leave the ant nest to search for help.
9. No, they are not actually warriors.
10. Talking it out
11. Yes
12. No
13. They are in the Green Zone. They are feeling good and calm about their situation.
14. That the bugs are not there to perform their circus act, they realize that they are there to fight the grasshoppers.
15. He is in the Yellow Zone—he is worried and upset about learning that the bugs are not warriors.
16. Social Fake
17. They feel betrayed by Flik and feel that they are doomed when the grasshoppers return.
18. They get happy and excited as well.
19. He is trying to distract the grasshopper by making him angry.
20. At first they were annoyed with Flik. At the end, they feel he is a hero and they respect and appreciate him.
21. Yes
22. He helps them stand up to the grasshoppers and keep their food.
23. [answers will vary]

Toy Story 3 Film Study Answer Key

Day #1:

1. Scared
2. Loved
3. Outgrew
4. Normal
5. Empathy
6. [opinion]

Day #2:

1. Happy
2. Crush, they are looking at each other, smiling and being flirty.
3. Andy
4. Bullied
5. Lotso
6. Negative thoughts

Day #3:

1. You can tell because of his nonverbals, facial expressions, and overall body language. He is slumping his shoulders, frowning, and looking down.
2. When the children play too rough with the toys, they feel upset, scared, and tired.
3. Nervous
4. Happy
5. Scared

Day #4:

1. Bad thoughts
2. Sad
3. Does not
4. Sad
5. Does

Day #5:

1. Surprised
2. He smiles at her, gives her a flower, and asks her to dance/dances with her.
3. [answers will vary]

The Angry Birds Movie Film Study Answer Key

Day #1:

1. [answers will vary]
2. Outside, below
3. Below
4. Thought
5. Green
6. Calming

Day #2:

1. Angry
2. Green
3. Above
4. Unexpected
5. Outside voice
6. Quiet/inside voice
7. [answers will vary]

Day #3:

1. Yellow
2. Below
3. [answers will vary]
4. They are hurting the birds
5. Angry

Day #4:

1. Sorry
2. Choices
3. Mouth
4. Below
5. Blue
6. Above
7. Red, You need to Stop, Opt and Go!
8. [answers will vary]

ACKNOWLEDGMENTS AND COLLABORATIONS

UNIT 1: Friendships, Rapport Building, and Trust

- Lesson 4: Friendship Collage contributed by Molly Klonk
- Lesson 5: Lyric Analysis contributed by Molly Klonk

UNIT 3: Dealing with Setbacks and Change

- Lesson 2: Calming Plan strategies compiled in collaboration with Mary Yelton, Occupational Therapist, and Peyton Crosley, TPT
- Lesson 4: Bouncing Back was adapted by colleague and friend Marcia Harris, from "Skills to Pay the Bills" (National Parent Center on Transition and Employment, 2012)
- My Worry Journal template inspired by podcast episode titled "Back to School Panic" from *Losing 100 Pounds with Corinne* by Corinne Crabtree (Crabtree, 2020)

UNIT 4: Executive Functioning

- Lesson 5: Dear Teacher Letter adapted from contribution by Libby Casanova, Katy Hargrove-Schwieterman, and Heather Taylor

UNIT 5: It's All About Perspective

- Lesson 3: Silent Movie contributed by Molly Klonk

UNIT 6: Navigating Social Media in Middle School

- Lesson 3: Social Media Thoughts and Feelings contributed by Sarah Allworth
- Lesson 4: Cross the Line contributed by Molly Klonk

UNIT 7: Growing Up, Changing Rules, and Transition

- Lesson 5: Emotion Matching Game contributed by Rilie McKaig, M.S. CCC-SLP

UNIT 8: Using Film and Video Clips to Teach Social Skills

- *A Bug's Life* film study contributed by Sarah Allworth
- *Angry Birds* film study contributed by Marina Mendel
- Lesson 2: Suggested clips contributed by 2020–2021 PEERspective students at Beavercreek High School

Appendices

- Appendix 9 created in conjunction with Rilie McKaig, M.S. CCC-SLP. Originally published by AAPC Publishing (Schmidt, 2020c)
- Appendix 10 created in conjunction with Rilie McKaig, M.S. CCC-SLP. Originally published by AAPC Publishing (Schmidt, 2020c)

Artwork

- Mackenzie Binkis, 2019 PEERspective student, created the artwork for Parent Corner
- Alison Stonecypher, 2021 PEERspective student, created the artwork for Teacher Talk

TESTIMONIALS

"After Communications Class (PEERspective), I found it easier to make friends. I found the confidence to be myself and embrace my quirks."

—Mackenzie, Parent Corner artist

"This class has provided me with a better understanding of who I am as a person and has given me the confidence I need while speaking in a group setting. Honestly, Comm Class was my favorite part of the day because I know that in that class, I feel confident that I have a strong community of friends surrounding me."

—Ali, Teacher Talk artist

"The PEERspective Learning Approach curriculum is well organized, authentic, and easy to implement, allowing for any teacher who wants to start using PEERspective in their school to dive right in. Jen gives many helpful and experienced insights into working with students with social communication needs. She values the strengths of all students and the peer coach model is incredibly genuine and meaningful. I truly could not have started a Communications Class at my school without the resources that Jen provided."

—Alexandra Ray

"For the past four years as a speech-language pathologist, I have worked with a variety of students with social communication challenges by conducting direct small group instruction and indirect social groups such as lunch bunch and communication club. In 2018, I had the opportunity to attend an in-service in which Jennifer Schmidt presented a novel and intriguing way to assist students to transfer social communication and life skills learned in the classroom into the home, workplace, and community. I realized at the in-service that Jennifer's curriculum was the critical piece I had been looking for to further assist my students. It provides students with intentional instruction in a structured classroom setting but also allows students to develop and expand their social skills in more natural, authentic settings (e.g., school dances, basketball games, shopping at the mall). The PEERspective learning approach expands classroom instruction by incorporating field trips, social outings, and club activities into the curriculum. This class delivers a fun and enjoyable way for students to practice and expand their communication skills. For example, a student that may typically stay home on a Friday night playing video games alone will go with his/her peers and peer coaches to a football game, a bowling alley, or a restaurant to socially engage with others. The PEERspective curriculum utilizes over 20 evidence-based practices proven to be successful for students with autism spectrum disorders (ASD). This coming school year, I am excited to pilot the PEERspective curriculum with Pam Schultz, intervention specialist at Bellbrook High School. I hope to incorporate the PEERspective curriculum into our middle school in the future."

—Danielle Brodnick

"Taylor would be excited to have me come pick her up after school, but she would often be overwhelmed and would cry. The film study and Social Communication Class helped her recognize her emotion as happy and that her face and body needed to show that it was happy and not sad (to see me)."

—Jolene, parent
(Endorsement for the *Inside Out* Film Study, Unit 8)